On the Way to the
Promised Land

A Guided Discovery for Groups and Individuals

Kevin Perrotta

LOYOLAPRESS.
CHICAGO

LOYOLAPRESS.

3441 N. ASHLAND AVENUE
CHICAGO, ILLINOIS 60657
(800) 621-1008
WWW.LOYOLABOOKS.ORG

Nihil Obstat	*Imprimatur*
Reverend John G. Lodge, S.S.L., S.T.D.	Reverend George J. Rassas
Censor Deputatus	Vicar General
September 23, 2005	Archdiocese of Chicago
	September 26, 2005

The *Nihil Obstat* and *Imprimatur* are official declarations that a book is free of doctrinal and moral error. No implication is contained therein that those who have granted the *Nihil Obstat* and *Imprimatur* agree with the content, opinions, or statements expressed. Nor do they assume any legal responsibility associated with publication.

Interior design by Kay Hartmann/Communique Design
Illustration by Anni Betts

ISBN 0-8294-2248-X

Printed in the United States of America
06 07 08 09 10 11 Bang 10 9 8 7 6 5 4 3 2 1

Contents

How to Use This Guide

If you want to know how to respond to Jesus' invitation to follow him as his disciple, the natural place to begin is the Bible. Because the Holy Spirit guided the authors of Scripture, the book they wrote is an always-fresh source of wisdom on everything concerning God and our relationship with him.

In this book we will read about the Israelites' journey to the land God promised them, in order to learn from this story about our following Jesus. As we proceed, we will explore connections between what we find in Scripture and our own life. The goal is to grow in our response to Jesus' invitation to follow him as his disciples.

Our approach will be a *guided discovery*. It will be *guided* because we all need support in understanding Scripture and reflecting on what it means for our lives. Scripture was written to be understood and applied in the community of faith, so we read the Bible *for* ourselves but not *by* ourselves. Even if we are reading alone rather than in a group, we need resources that help us grow in understanding. Our approach is also one of *discovery,* because each of us needs to encounter Scripture for ourselves and consider its meaning for our life. No one can do this for us.

This book is designed to give you both guidance for understanding and tools for discovery.

The introduction on page 6 will guide your reading by providing background material and helping you get oriented to the subject of our exploration. Each week, a brief "Background" section will give you context for the reading, and the "Exploring the Theme" section that follows the reading will bring out the meaning of the Scripture passages. Supplementary material between sessions will offer further resources for understanding.

The main tool for discovery is the "Questions for Reflection and Discussion" section in each session. The first questions in this section are designed to spur you to notice things in the text, sharpen your powers of observation, and read for comprehension. Other questions suggest ways to compare the people, situations, and experiences in the biblical texts with your own life and the world today—an important step toward grasping what God is saying to you through the Scripture and what your response might be. Choose the questions you think will work best for you. Preparing to answer all the questions ahead of time is highly recommended.

We suggest that you pay particular attention to the final question each week, labeled "Focus question." This question points to an especially important issue raised by the reading. Do leave enough time for everyone in the group to discuss it!

Other sections encourage you to take an active approach to your Bible reading and discussion. At the start of each session, "Questions to Begin" will help you break the ice and start talk flowing. Often these questions are light and have only a slight connection to the reading. After each Scripture reading, there is a suggested time for a "First Impression." This gives you a chance to express a brief, initial, personal response to the text. Each session ends with a "Prayer to Close" that suggests a way of expressing your response to God.

How long are the discussion sessions? We've assumed you will have about an hour and twenty minutes. If you have less time, you'll find that most of the elements can be shortened somewhat.

Is homework necessary? You will get the most out of your discussions if you read the weekly material and prepare your answers to the questions in advance of each meeting. If participants are not able to prepare, read the "Exploring the Theme" sections aloud at the points where they appear.

What about leadership? You don't have to be an expert in the Bible to lead a discussion. Choose one or two people to act as discussion facilitators, and have everyone in the group read "Suggestions for Bible Discussion Groups" (page 92) before beginning.

Does everyone need a guide? a Bible? Everyone in the group will need their own copy of this book. It contains the biblical texts, so a Bible is not absolutely necessary—but each person will find it useful to have one. You should have at least one Bible on hand for your discussions. (See page 96 for recommendations.)

Before you begin, take a look at the suggestions for Bible discussion groups (page 92) or individuals (page 95).

Lessons from a Trip

If you visit Rome, you will find churches adorned with brilliant mosaics and frescoes of biblical scenes, Jesus, and the saints. Under some of the oldest churches, you will also find excavations. There, archaeologists have uncovered plain brick-and-concrete walls—remnants of houses, apartments, warehouses, factories, and shops from the first, second, and third centuries. Christians gathered in these homes and workplaces during this early period because they could not build churches. Christianity was illegal, and Christians were sometimes fiercely persecuted. When the emperor Constantine legalized Christianity, around the year 300, Christians began to erect churches above these sites where they had already been meeting.

With their plain brick walls below and spectacular artwork above, these churches testify to the life of the Church in two eras. In the earlier period, many men and women whose names are unknown to us—and whose lives were as ordinary as the unadorned walls of their dwellings—followed Jesus faithfully, some of them even to the point of a martyr's death. In the face of misunderstanding and hostility, these early believers shared the gospel with people around them, and the Church grew. After Constantine, the Christians who began to build beautiful churches also began to build the gospel into their society. Little by little, they shaped a culture that at least to some degree acknowledged God's providence and presence and recognized the demands of justice and the dignity of the weakest members.

To visit these Roman churches is to be reminded of the debt of gratitude we owe all these Christians of earlier times. With the help of the Holy Spirit, they passed on the gospel to us and left us a rich heritage. There is an important similarity between these earlier Christians and us. Just as the Christian faith has come to us through them, so it will reach later generations through us. Hopefully, people in the future will thank God that we Christians of the twenty-first century responded to Jesus' call and handed on to them a world touched by his grace.

Between us and the Roman Christians in the time of Constantine there is a further parallel. Like them, we seem to be passing from one era to another. Amid great technological, economic, political, and cultural changes, we have entered a new millennium that presents fresh opportunities for the gospel to reach men and women throughout the world, as well as new obstacles and problems.

As we face the challenges of our new era, it is natural for us to look within our heritage as a Church for helpful resources. Among the most valuable is sacred Scripture—God's old but ever-present word to us. As Christian readers, we turn our attention primarily to the New Testament, where we find Jesus and the early Church. But if we look behind Jesus and his first disciples at the portion of the Bible that was Scripture for them—the Old Testament—we will also find much that is useful. Especially instructive for a Church traveling into a new era are the accounts of the Israelite people's great trek from Egypt to Canaan—an account that fills the books of Exodus, Leviticus, Numbers, and Deuteronomy. Theirs was a journey from slavery to freedom, a journey on which God revealed himself to them, drew them into a relationship with himself, and formed them as a people. These events were foundational for the people of Israel. And they stand as the model of God's dealings with us as followers of his Son. The Church, the community of those who are baptized into Christ, continues to travel from the slavery of sin to the freedom of love. God's revelation of himself to the Israelites foreshadowed God's greater revelation of himself to all men and women in Jesus. The covenant that God gave the Israelites foreshadowed the more intimate relationship with himself that God now offers to all through Jesus. The miracles by which God sustained the Israelites on their journey foreshadowed his presence with us in Jesus and in his Spirit, and, in a particular way, in the Eucharist. Thus, referring to the Israelites' experiences on their journey, the apostle Paul tells us, "These things happened to them to serve as an example, and they were written down to instruct us, on whom the ends of the ages have come" (1 Corinthians 10:11). In this guide, then, we will read about the Israelites' great journey, seeking the instruction it contains for us.

Jacob
Joseph - son of Jacob

Who were the Israelites? What was the purpose of their journey? The Israelites' ancestors were a small group of shepherds in the ancient Near East who went to Egypt to escape a famine and then stayed on. Their descendants became enslaved by the government. The men were forced to make bricks for building projects. The Bible does not name the Egyptian kings, called pharaohs, who oppressed the Israelites, but one of them, it seems, was Rameses II, an especially powerful pharaoh who ruled Egypt during the thirteenth century before Christ. Rameses commissioned the construction of an enormous city in the Nile Delta, and named it Rameses, after himself. A modern archaeologist who has been excavating the ruins of Rameses says that after forty years of digging he has only *begun* to uncover the ancient city. He estimates that the city of Rameses was some four square miles—huge by ancient standards, and requiring a heck of a lot of bricks!

The Israelites suffered in their enslavement, and God paid attention to their situation. He commissioned an Israelite named Moses to confront the pharaoh and to lead the Israelites to freedom. Aided by miraculous displays of divine power, Moses did just that. He brought the twelve tribes of Israelites out of the Nile Delta. When the escaping slaves encountered a body of water blocking their way, and the pharaoh's army was coming up behind them, God staged a spectacular rescue, bringing the Israelites safely through the water. Moses then led the people east into the Sinai Peninsula. At Mount Sinai, God formally established a relationship with the people and gave them instructions for a way of life based on justice and compassion. (An earlier Six Weeks book, entitled *God to the Rescue,* offers a guide to this earlier portion of the story.)

It is at this point, with the Israelites encamped at Mount Sinai, that our readings in the present book begin. Over the next six weeks, we will follow the Israelites as they set out from Mount Sinai and travel north into the Negev, a desert area that is today in the south of the modern state of Israel. From the Negev they head east, then north, into what is now the kingdom of Jordan. Their journey will end on the east side of the Jordan River, where they will camp across from Jericho, preparing to cross over into Canaan—present-day Israel and Palestine.

The journey involved radical, probably terrifying, changes for the Israelites. The Nile Delta, where they had been living, was and is flat, moist, and lush—today the ruins of the city of Rameses lie beneath rice fields. Waterfowl and fish live in the canals. But the delta is an oasis in a vast desert. Vegetation abruptly ends at the edge of the area watered by the Nile. As soon as the Israelites left the delta, they found themselves in an unfamiliar wasteland. In the Sinai Peninsula, they encountered a wilderness of towering granite mountains and rock-strewn valleys under a blazing sun. Depending on the lay of the land and the composition of the rocks, the temperature rises to extremes that bring rapid dehydration and death. The difficulties of travel through such terrain are obvious. The scarcity of water was an immediate and constant problem. In the Sinai, one travels from oasis to oasis. The Israelites needed guidance to find the oases—and to stay clear of treacherous slopes where loose rocks may suddenly slide away under travelers' feet. For people who had spent their lives in the muddy, green Nile Delta, the barren, jagged Sinai wilderness was a difficult and dangerous place.

The wilderness put the Israelites under pressure, and the effects of the pressure begin to appear in our reading in Week 1. Moses climbs Mount Sinai to receive instructions from God and remains for weeks at the top of the mountain. Not having any indication of what has happened to him, the people below become restless. They resort to a means of coping with their anxiety that provokes a crisis in their relationship with God. A complete rupture is only narrowly averted. Once the relationship is restored, the Israelites get organized for their trip and set out—our readings in Week 2. But almost immediately, physical hardships provoke them to complaints and rebellion (Week 3). Envy causes further disarray (Week 4).

After a while, God brings the Israelites to the southern border of Canaan and tells them to enter. Fearing the people who already live there, however, the Israelites refuse. In fact, they make plans to return to Egypt. (The incident is told in Numbers 13–14.) God responds with anger tinged with disappointment: "How long will this people despise me? And how long will they refuse to believe in me, in spite of all the signs that I have done among them?" (Numbers 14:11). Moses intercedes for the people, and God forgives them. But their cowardice and lack of trust in God have consequences: God condemns them to go on wandering in the wilderness for an entire generation, until those who escaped from slavery in Egypt die. Their children will enter the land God has promised to give them. Thus a trip that could have taken a few months stretches out to forty years.

The barren Sinai Peninsula and Negev desert are sparsely populated. But in the hill country east of the Dead Sea and the Jordan River, the Israelites find villages and cities. Problems inevitably arise with the local inhabitants, as we see in Week 5. First there is a military confrontation. Then the Israelites fall under the influence of the local people's religion.

Finally, beside the Jordan River, Moses delivers a farewell sermon to the people. Afterward he climbs a hill from which he can look west over the river valley to the land of Canaan, and dies (Week 6). The Israelites' entry into the land—and their continuing journey through the centuries—is recorded in the historical books of the Old Testament.

We get to know both God and the Israelites better as we read about their interactions on the journey. The people's many needs and their lack of cooperation with God provide frequent opportunities for God to demonstrate his helpfulness and patience, and also to communicate his insistence on being trusted and obeyed. Tracing the emerging portrait of God is one of the chief interests in reading the accounts of the journey.

The Israelites learn about God as they go. Back in Egypt, they probably had some traditional stories about God's dealings with their ancestors, but they do not seem to have a close relationship with him when he intervenes on their behalf against Pharaoh (see Exodus 5, especially verse 21). Because they do not know him very well, God does not at first expect a high level of faith from them. For example, when they run out of water and food soon after escaping from Egypt, they complain despairingly, but God does not reproach them for their lack of faith; he just provides what they need (Exodus 15:22–16:36). Over time, however, as the Israelites experience his care, God expects them to grow in faith. As readers we may observe their growth—and failure to grow—and may ask ourselves how we are like them.

The strange environment through which the Israelites travel presents them with a range of challenges. They leave behind the familiar flora and fauna of the Nile Delta and now awake each day to unfamiliar sounds and smells. Their diet changes. No more fish! Their work changes, too. No longer having to make mud bricks from dawn to dusk is a relief, but now they have to learn how to tend sheep and goats in a wilderness of sparse vegetation. In every respect, they are wrenched out of old ways and forced into new ones. Their reactions to this demand give us food for thought about our own willingness to relate well to change.

The changes required of the Israelites involve more than a new menu and different work. The people go from being made to work as slaves, but being supplied with food, to being free of overseers, yet having to provide for their own needs. Released from slavery, they must learn to take responsibility for themselves. Thus, what starts out as a journey from slavery to freedom becomes a journey from freedom to freedom: given freedom from injustice, oppression, exploitation, and racism by the Egyptians, they must now seek freedom from their own old habits, expectations, and fears. By rescuing them and giving them his laws, God gives them the opportunity to lead a dignified life of justice and mutual responsibility. But to take hold of this opportunity, they must resist doubts and fears and put their trust in him. Until they can stand up to the allurements and threats they meet on the way, they will not be able to receive God's promises. Will they take responsibility for responding to God's invitation amid difficulties? Or will they become impatient, indulge in complaints, and blame others for their problems? As we follow their story, we will see much of ourselves reflected in these former slaves.

As Christians, we read about the Israelites' journey through the lens of faith in Jesus. Our own journey is a journey with him. The home toward which he is leading us is not the territory between the Jordan River and the Mediterranean Sea but the kingdom of God. Unlike Canaan, toward which the Israelites traveled, God's kingdom is not just up ahead of us but is already present, in Jesus. Despite these differences, however, the Israelites' journey is, as St. Paul says, instructive for us, for it brings to light a lot about God and about human beings that remains true and relevant for our journey with Jesus.

I should warn you that there are some distasteful elements in the accounts we will read. For example, God is sometimes said to send plagues as a punishment for people's sins. This raises theological and historical questions that are too knotty for us to try to untangle here. It is, however, helpful to realize that in these Old Testament accounts we see God and the world through the eyes of people who lived in a culture much different from ours. They accepted a kind of "after, therefore, because of" reasoning: if a plague came after a sin, the sin was regarded as the cause of the plague, which was viewed as punishment for the sin. There are shortcomings in this way of thinking, but they do not detract from the basic message of the biblical accounts. What the biblical authors regarded as sin is indeed sin, and sin is harmful, even if it is not the immediate cause of disasters. The biblical authors' "after, therefore, because of" reasoning was to be corrected in the process of God's revelation of himself. The book of Job marks one stage in this process. Jesus' teaching marks a further stage. Jesus remarked that a man's blindness was *not* a punishment for sin (John 9:1–3). By the same token, plagues, earthquakes, tsunamis, droughts, and so on should not be interpreted as punishments, although they may be taken as images for the toll that sin exacts (see Luke 13:1–5).

In one of our readings, God commends an Israelite named Phinehas for acting in a murderous rage against an Israelite who publicly flaunted idolatrous behavior (Numbers 25—Week 5). We may wonder how such an action could be acceptable to the God who has revealed himself in Jesus. Here it is useful to realize that God revealed himself to the people of Israel in a progressive way, leading them from a partial and incomplete understanding of him to a fuller knowledge. Texts such as Numbers 25 are evidence of the process. Such passages raise questions about the manner in which God adapted his word to the Israelites' understanding. What was God's real message to them? How well did they grasp what he was saying to them? Exploring these questions would take us far beyond the scope of this book. But the basic principle by which we proceed as followers of Jesus is clear. When we encounter Old Testament texts that present a message about God and his will that falls short of or diverges from the example and teaching of Jesus, we interpret those texts as somehow a partial preparation for Jesus or a prefigurement of him. Thus, for example, it seems possible to find in the Phinehas story not a divine affirmation of religious violence but an authentic message about the fundamental importance God places on people recognizing him alone as the source of life and about the value of an individual taking action to help the community of believers recognize this truth.

While we can learn from the Israelites' journey through the wilderness, we will not, of course, find specific answers in the biblical accounts for our twenty-first-century problems. We will, however, find profound insights into God and ourselves. And the readings will spur us to ask questions about our relationships with God and with one another. The Israelites' long trip through the wilderness brought them to a greater state of readiness to enter the land where God wished them to dwell. Reading about their journey can help us move forward together in the new millennium that God has begun to give us—and to use it well.

AN AWESOME THING

Questions to Begin

10 minutes
Use a question or two to get warmed up for the reading.

Wedding Ring

1 What's your favorite piece of jewelry?

2 When have you been more impressed by seeing or encountering something than by just hearing or reading about it?

With kids @ school.

3 Can you remember a time when you were impatient but later regretted it?

At that time they made a calf, offered a sacrifice to the idol, and reveled in the works of their hands.

Acts 7:41

Opening the Bible

10 minutes
Read the passage aloud. Let individuals take turns reading
paragraphs.

The Background

The Israelites are camping next to Mount Sinai, in the Sinai wilderness, where God has established a covenant—a formal relationship—with them. God has summoned Moses to climb the mountain to receive further instructions. Moses has gone up the mountain and stayed for forty days (Exodus 24:18)—a number that, in the Bible, implies a period of time set aside by God for a special purpose. But to the people who are waiting in the camp, Moses' absence does not feel like part of a carefully scheduled divine plan.

The Reading: Exodus 32:1–16, 19–24, 30–34; 33:3–4, 12, 15–23; 34:1, 4–11, 28

The Calm Above, the Turmoil Below

Exodus 32:1 When the people saw that Moses delayed to come down from the mountain, the people gathered around Aaron, and said to him, "Come, make gods for us, who shall go before us; as for this Moses, the man who brought us up out of the land of Egypt, we do not know what has become of him." 2 Aaron said to them, "Take off the gold rings that are on the ears of your wives, your sons, and your daughters, and bring them to me." 3 So all the people took off the gold rings from their ears, and brought them to Aaron. 4 He took the gold from them, formed it in a mold, and cast an image of a calf; and they said, "These are your gods, O Israel, who brought you up out of the land of Egypt!"

5 When Aaron saw this, he built an altar before it; and Aaron made proclamation and said, "Tomorrow shall be a festival to the LORD." 6 They rose early the next day, and offered burnt offerings and brought sacrifices of well-being; and the people sat down to eat and drink, and rose up to revel.

7 The LORD said to Moses, "Go down at once! Your people, whom you brought up out of the land of Egypt, have acted perversely; 8 they have been quick to turn aside from the way that I commanded them; they have cast for themselves an image of a calf, and have worshiped it and sacrificed to it, and said, 'These are your gods, O Israel, who brought you up out of the land of Egypt!'" 9 The LORD

said to Moses, "I have seen this people, how stiff-necked they are. [10] Now let me alone, so that my wrath may burn hot against them and I may consume them; and of you I will make a great nation."

[11] But Moses implored the LORD his God, and said, "O LORD, why does your wrath burn hot against your people, whom you brought out of the land of Egypt with great power and with a mighty hand? [12] Why should the Egyptians say, 'It was with evil intent that he brought them out to kill them in the mountains, and to consume them from the face of the earth'? Turn from your fierce wrath; change your mind and do not bring disaster on your people. [13] Remember Abraham, Isaac, and Israel, your servants, how you swore to them by your own self, saying to them, 'I will multiply your descendants like the stars of heaven, and all this land that I have promised I will give to your descendants, and they shall inherit it forever.'" [14] And the LORD changed his mind about the disaster that he planned to bring on his people.

[15] Then Moses turned and went down from the mountain, carrying the two tablets of the covenant in his hands, tablets that were written on both sides, written on the front and on the back. [16] The tablets were the work of God, and the writing was the writing of God, engraved upon the tablets. . . .

[19] As soon as he came near the camp and saw the calf and the dancing, Moses' anger burned hot, and he threw the tablets from his hands and broke them at the foot of the mountain. [20] He took the calf that they had made, burned it with fire, ground it to powder, scattered it on the water, and made the Israelites drink it.

[21] Moses said to Aaron, "What did this people do to you that you have brought so great a sin upon them?"

[22] And Aaron said, "Do not let the anger of my lord burn hot; you know the people, that they are bent on evil. [23] They said to me, 'Make us gods, who shall go before us; as for this Moses, the man who brought us up out of the land of Egypt, we do not know what has become of him.' [24] So I said to them, 'Whoever has gold, take it off'; so they gave it to me, and I threw it into the fire, and out came this calf!" . . .

Moses Goes Up the Mountain Again

[30] On the next day Moses said to the people, "You have sinned a great sin. But now I will go up to the LORD; perhaps I can make atonement for your sin."

31 So Moses returned to the LORD and said, "Alas, this people has sinned a great sin; they have made for themselves gods of gold. 32 But now, if you will only forgive their sin—but if not, blot me out of the book that you have written." 33 But the LORD said to Moses, "Whoever has sinned against me I will blot out of my book. 34 But now go, lead the people to the place about which I have spoken to you; see, my angel shall go in front of you. Nevertheless, when the day comes for punishment, I will punish them for their sin. . . . 33:3 Go up to a land flowing with milk and honey; but I will not go up among you, or I would consume you on the way, for you are a stiff-necked people."

4 When the people heard these harsh words, they mourned, and no one put on ornaments. . . .

Moses Talks with God at the Foot of the Mountain

12 Moses said to the LORD . . . 15 "If your presence will not go, do not carry us up from here. 16 For how shall it be known that I have found favor in your sight, I and your people, unless you go with us?" . . .

17 The LORD said to Moses, "I will do the very thing that you have asked; for you have found favor in my sight, and I know you by name." 18 Moses said, "Show me your glory, I pray." 19 And he said, "I will make all my goodness pass before you, and will proclaim before you the name, 'The LORD'; and I will be gracious to whom I will be gracious, and will show mercy on whom I will show mercy. 20 But," he said, "you cannot see my face; for no one shall see me and live." 21 And the LORD continued, "See, there is a place by me where you shall stand on the rock; 22 and while my glory passes by I will put you in a cleft of the rock, and I will cover you with my hand until I have passed by; 23 then I will take away my hand, and you shall see my back; but my face shall not be seen."

Moses Climbs the Mountain Once More

34:1 The LORD said to Moses, "Cut two tablets of stone like the former ones, and I will write on the tablets the words that were on the former tablets, which you broke. . . ." 4 So Moses cut two tablets of stone like the former ones; and he rose early in the morning and went up on Mount Sinai, as the LORD had commanded him, and took in his hand the two tablets of stone.

⁵ The LORD descended in the cloud and stood with him there, and proclaimed the name, "The LORD." ⁶ The LORD passed before him, and proclaimed,

"The LORD, the LORD,
a God merciful and gracious,
slow to anger,
and abounding in steadfast love and faithfulness,
⁷ keeping steadfast love for the thousandth generation,
forgiving iniquity and transgression and sin,
yet by no means clearing the guilty,
but visiting the iniquity of the parents
upon the children
and the children's children,
to the third and the fourth generation."

⁸ And Moses quickly bowed his head toward the earth, and worshiped. ⁹ He said, "If now I have found favor in your sight, O Lord, I pray, let the Lord go with us. Although this is a stiff-necked people, pardon our iniquity and our sin, and take us for your inheritance."

¹⁰ He said: I hereby make a covenant. Before all your people I will perform marvels, such as have not been performed in all the earth or in any nation; and all the people among whom you live shall see the work of the LORD; for it is an awesome thing that I will do with you. ¹¹ Observe what I command you today. . . .

²⁸ He was there with the LORD forty days and forty nights; he neither ate bread nor drank water. And he wrote on the tablets the words of the covenant, the ten commandments.

First Impression

5 minutes
Briefly mention a question you have about the reading or one thing in it that surprised, impressed, delighted, or challenged you. No discussion! Just listen to one another's reactions.

If participants have not read this section already, read it aloud.
Otherwise go on to "Questions for Reflection and Discussion."

32:1–6. Moses has been the Israelites' go-between with God and their guide in the wilderness. His absence arouses anxieties. If Moses has abandoned them, who will show them the way? They feel the need to replace him with a new means for being in contact with God. They meet the need by making a metal statue of a bull.

It was common for people in the ancient Near East to picture a god standing on a bull, which symbolized strength. Probably the Israelites regard their bull statue, too, as a pedestal for God, who, they imagine, stands invisibly upon it. They seem to regard the statue not as a replacement for God but as a symbol of his presence. This, at least, is how Aaron relates to it. He welcomes the bull as a manifestation of the God who has brought the people out of Egypt. In Hebrew, the same word stands for both *God* and *gods,* so the people's acclamation of the bull as the *gods* who brought them out of Egypt sounds like an acknowledgment of the *God* who brought them out. Notice that God does not accuse the people of turning to *other* gods but of using a statue of a bull in their worship (32:8). This violates his first command to them (20:4).

Symbolizing God with a bull might seem to express confidence in his power. But there are problems with this approach. It implies that God is part of nature rather than its creator. Thus demoted, God would be subject to other natural forces—perhaps even subject to the demands of his worshipers. They might consider their image of him as a kind of lever by which to get him to provide the goods and services they desire. The slide from worship to magic would begin.

In addition, the bull image harkens back to the religion of Egypt, with its numerous animal-like gods. Those gods reflected a false value system. They supported the pharaoh and his dictatorial regime, which oppressed other peoples, such as the Israelites. Unlike those gods, the God who has revealed himself to Israel never supports injustice. He is on the side of the underdog, as he has demonstrated to the Israelites. So they should avoid representing him in a way that tends to confuse him with the gods who support an unjust social order.

The Israelites offer sacrifices before the bull statue, hoping to strengthen their relationship with God (32:6). God would prefer them to obey his instructions (see 1 Samuel 15:22). After eating the remainder of the sacrificial food, they begin to "revel" (32:6). The Hebrew word refers to dancing (Judges 16:25, where it is sometimes translated "entertain") and sexual activity (Genesis 26:8, sometimes translated "fondling"; 39:14, 17, sometimes translated "insult").

32:7–14. Up on the mountain, God has been giving Moses instructions for constructing a shrine that will be the focal point for his presence among the people (Exodus 25–31). There is no point in continuing the instructions now that the people, in their impatience, have made their own focal point for God's presence—one that violates their relationship with him.

The people are "stiff-necked," God says (32:9)—not teachable, unwilling to change their ways of thinking and acting. God declares his intention to punish them (32:10). Why, then, does he ask Moses to step aside? St. Gregory the Great remarked that it is almost as if God wishes Moses to hold him back. It would be a mistake to see here a struggle between divine vengeance and human mercy. After all, Moses is God's servant. God chose him. And God implicitly invites him to intercede for the people. In fact, Moses expresses what is in God's mind. The interplay of justice and mercy within God is made visible by being projected outward into a conversation between God and his human servant.

God responds positively to Moses' pleading (32:14). Biblical scholar R. W. L. Moberly comments: "It is God's faithfulness alone which is the basis for forgiveness; and yet this faithfulness is only revealed and made actual when Moses' bold intercession calls it forth." To intercede on behalf of others, as Moses does, is to enter into the heart of God and play a role in the unfolding of God's purposes in others' lives.

In his appeal (32:11–13), Moses does not minimize the people's offense or argue that their good deeds outweigh their sin. He appeals to God's loving intentions. "You decided long ago to show your mercy," he argues. "Well, continue to do so!" Moses recognizes that God can fulfill his good promises to human beings only if he is willing to practice constant mercy and forgiveness, because we humans constantly fail to cooperate with God's plans. St. Paul will make the same point (see Romans 4:13–15).

32:15–24. For Moses, hearing about the Israelites' unfaithfulness is one thing; seeing it is another (32:19). By angrily shattering the stone tablets, he signals that the covenant between God and the people is broken. Moses' strange requirement that the people drink water containing the pulverized statue (32:20) may be part of a trial by ordeal designed to identify the guilty parties (compare Numbers 5:12–31) so that the punishment (32:25–29) falls only on them.

Aaron excuses his own behavior and shifts the blame onto the people (32:22–24). His only concern is to escape punishment. Apparently he would be happy to see the people punished for their sin. What a contrast with Moses! Moses cares less for himself than for the people. He is willing to stand with them to shield them from punishment, even though it would be to his own advantage to stand aside (32:10–11). Yet for reasons unexplained, Aaron escapes punishment.

32:30–34. Moses persuaded God to relent (32:14), but nothing was said about forgiveness. So Moses now seeks complete restoration of the relationship between God and the people. Like a heartbroken parent praying for a wayward child, Moses prays for the Israelites, declaring that if God will not fully restore his relationship with the people, he has no further interest in living (32:31–32).

God's response is ambiguous (32:33). It can be interpreted as making no concession: Israel has sinned; all will be punished. Or as a partial concession: God will punish the ringleaders but will be merciful to those who were only indirectly involved in the idolatry. Or as a complete concession: since Moses, who has not sinned, identifies himself with the people, God will not destroy the people, for he will not destroy Moses. Whatever interpretation one is inclined to accept, God's words are less than a declaration of forgiveness. The Israelites remain under a cloud of guilt.

33:3–4. God offers to guide the people—from a distance. If he were "among" them, their sins would provoke his anger (33:3). This is not a denial that God is present everywhere but a way of expressing the chasm that separates God from sin. The announcement of God's aloofness grieves the Israelites (33:4), although their response falls short of a clear-cut acknowledgement of their sin.

33:12–23. In Moses' eyes, being guided through the wilderness, even getting settled in the land of Canaan, is not enough. The important thing about being God's people is having a personal relationship with God. What are God's gifts worth without God? So Moses seeks God's presence with the people—and the forgiveness that makes reconciliation possible.

Moses seems to achieve his purpose (33:17). Yet he knows the people are still prone to sin. If they start out on the journey with God in their midst and fall into further rebellion, will a worse punishment befall them? Moses feels the need of a further revelation of God's mercy to undergird the relationship between God and the people. This, it seems, is why Moses asks God to reveal himself (33:18). By asking to see God's "glory," Moses is asking to see God in his goodness and mercy.

In his answer, God speaks of his "goodness" (33:19) and his "glory" (33:22), which seem to be identical with himself, since all will pass before Moses (33:23). God is glorious, splendid, majestic, blindingly radiant—yet his glory is not raw power but goodness. At the same time, God makes it clear that there is freedom and mystery in him: "I will be gracious to whom I will be gracious" (33:19). There is nothing mechanical about God's mercy, nothing on which we can presume. Furthermore, God's revelation of himself to Moses is limited because Moses is limited: no human being, no matter how highly favored, can know God completely (33:20–23). Among human beings, only Jesus knows God fully, for he is God's Son (John 1:18; 14:9).

34:1–11, 28. The idea of God standing with Moses seems odd (34:5). But the Hebrew can be interpreted as meaning that *God* came down and *Moses* stood in his presence.

God proclaims his name—the enigmatic Hebrew word is here translated "the Lord"—and spells out its meaning (34:6–7). In other words, God declares the kind of person he is. God is merciful, even if humans are not. God is forgiving to human beings, who continually fall into sin. Verse 7 seems to express a contradiction: the forgiving God does not forgive. But a rabbinic interpretation—"He remits punishment for the penitent, but not for the impenitent"—is probably on the right track. In any case, the note of judgment sounded here puts us on notice that we cannot blithely go on sinning on the assumption that God will automatically forgive us—the attitude captured in German poet Heinrich Heine's supposed deathbed pronouncement: "God will forgive me. It's his job."

In the presence of the merciful God, Moses asks God to forgive the Israelites and live in their midst again ("let the Lord go with us"—34:9). In Moses' appeal, the "although" could be translated "because"; that is, *because* the people are sinful, God should be forgiving! In Moses' view, God is so loving that the sight of our sins draws from him a response of compassion, just as a physician is spurred to action by the sight of an injured person being wheeled into the ER.

God's incomprehensible mercy will be the foundation of the Israelites' relationship with him on their journey. They will still be sinners, but God's mercy will be greater than their sins. Mercy will make possible an ongoing relationship between the good God and the people who often fail to be good. The "awesome thing" that God will do (34:10) is to have an ongoing covenant relationship with sinners. His acts of forgiveness toward the Israelites will be "marvels" (34:10) greater than the miracles by which he set them free from slavery.

Earlier, the Israelites self-confidently declared, "All that the Lord has spoken we will do" (24:7). They know themselves better now. And they know God better. They have learned that he is serious about being obeyed, yet also merciful when they disobey. They will march away from Mount Sinai not as a people proudly able to proclaim their loyalty to God. Rather they will set forth under a banner proclaiming, "The Lord, a God merciful and gracious" (34:6).

As the Church, we too go forward into the new millennium under the banner of divine mercy, emblazoned with the cross of Jesus Christ. We present ourselves to the world not as paragons of virtue but as men and women who have experienced God's forgiveness—and invite others to experience it.

Questions for Reflection and Discussion

45 minutes
Choose questions according to your interest and time.

1 Compare the statements about who led the Israelites out of Egypt and whose people the Israelites are in 32:7 and 11. How do you explain the differences?

2 Reread 32:7–8. What do you think God expects Moses to do when he goes down the mountain?

3 In 32:1, the people seem to assume that God is absent. How do God's statements in 32:7–8 refute this assumption?

4 Compare Aaron's account of events (32:22–24) with the biblical author's account (32:1–5). Where does Aaron's account follow the author's? Where does it diverge? Why? What opinion of Aaron do you form from this?

5 When, like Aaron, have you gone along with something wrong at school, in your family, at work? What did you learn from the experience?

6 Reread 34:6–7. God describes himself as "merciful," "gracious," "slow to anger," "abounding in steadfast love," and "forgiving." In your relationships with people, how have you learned the meaning of these words? How much can a person understand these words if he or she does not express these qualities? How is God calling you to embody these qualities in a relationship with someone in your life?

7 What kinds of things can we know about God? In what ways does he exceed our ability to know him? What has helped you to know God? What has helped you realize that God is greater than you can understand? How can a person develop a true picture of who God is and what he is like? What role does Scripture play in this? What role does the Church play?

8 When has God kept you waiting? What are you waiting for now? Are you trusting God in the meantime?

9 Do you ever wish to see people suffer for the wrong they have done? Do you pray that God will show them mercy? In this regard, are you more like Aaron or like Moses?

10 Can sin and repentance be a route to a deeper knowledge of God?

11 What qualities of good leadership does Moses demonstrate? How could you imitate him in some situation in your own life?

12 For Personal Reflection: Do you ever try to relieve your anxieties with something false or destructive? What would be a more constructive way of dealing with anxiety? Do you turn to God for help when you are anxious?

13 **Focus question.** How have you experienced God's mercy? Is God's mercy to you something you let other people know about? How do you reflect God's mercy in your relationships with other people? What opportunity do you have this week to show mercy? How does the Church bring the news of God's mercy to the world? How do you contribute to it?

10 minutes
Use this approach—or create your own!

◆ Pray together: "O God, you are gracious, slow to anger, and abounding in steadfast love and faithfulness. You never stop forgiving sins and showing mercy."

Leader: "For our impatience,"
Group: "Forgive us, Lord."
Leader: "For our idolatry,"
Group: "Forgive us, Lord."
Leader: "For our failures to take responsibility for our sins,"
Group: "Forgive us, Lord."
Leader: "Because we are stiff-necked,"
Group: "Have mercy, Lord."
Leader: "On our families and all who are close to us,"
Group: "Have mercy, Lord."
Leader: "On all our neighbors, near and far,"
Group: "Have mercy, Lord."
Leader: "On those who have hurt us,"
Group: "Have mercy, Lord."

End by praying together Psalm 89:1–2 or an Our Father.

Between Discussions

A Messenger of Mercy

Moses acted as intercessor on behalf of the Israelites at Mount Sinai and, as we will see in further readings, he continues to do so on their journey through the wilderness. In this way, Moses foreshadowed Jesus Christ, who offered his life on a cross to reconcile the human race to God. Jesus was the perfect intercessor with God—a role he continues to fulfill on our behalf (see Romans 8:34; Hebrews 7:25; 1 John 2:1). But the completeness of Jesus' intercession does not eliminate the opportunity for others to intercede with God. On the contrary, Jesus shares his intercession with us. He invites us to participate in his redeeming love by entering into his offering of himself to the Father on behalf of all. In the history of the Church, some men and women have responded to this invitation to such a degree that they stand as models for the rest of us, reminders of our calling. In the twentieth century, one such person was Helena Kowalska.

Helena was born in 1905 in a village near Lodz, Poland. At the age of nineteen, she entered a convent in Warsaw. She did not have much formal education, and her health was poor, so the directors of the convent assigned her simple tasks such as cooking, answering the door, and taking care of the vegetable garden. But there was more than met the eye with Helena, now called Sister Faustina.

In the first few years after she entered the convent, Faustina went through a period when praying, even thinking about God, became difficult. She felt rejected by God. Those who gave her spiritual advice could recognize the common pattern of testing that God often uses to deepen the trust of those who seek him. Through this dark time, Faustina developed a profound sense of her smallness as a creature in the face of God's immensity. At the same time, her desire for God and her determination to obey him grew. She tried to be of service—and to be a source of cheer—to others in the little ways possible within the restrictions of convent life.

From the time she was seven, Faustina had occasionally heard Jesus speak to her. Now, after several years in the convent, she had a vision of Jesus. He was standing before her in a white robe, with rays of white and red light shining from his chest. She asked him what this vision meant. The bands of light, he told her, symbolized his love, which sets sinners right with God and fills them with God's life. He told her that he wished her to have the vision painted and publicly displayed as a reminder of his mercy. He also told her that he wished the Church to focus on God's mercy by establishing an annual Feast of Divine Mercy. The picture and the feast would emphasize the openness of his invitation to everyone to experience God's forgiveness and grace. "Let the sinner not be afraid to approach me," he told Faustina.

Jesus also gave Faustina instructions for a set of simple prayers to be repeated with the help of rosary beads. This "Chaplet of Divine Mercy" consists of the Our Father, the Hail Mary, the Apostles' Creed, and three brief prayers that offer Christ to the Father in atonement for sins, plead for God's mercy for the world, and adore God as holy, mighty, and ever-living.

Through a priest to whom she described her vision of the white-robed Jesus, Faustina made contact with an artist who painted what she had seen. The painting was first displayed in 1934. Through her priest friend, the message about devoting one Sunday each year to the celebration of God's mercy was relayed to Pope Pius XI—without any papal response.

The revelation strengthened Faustina's focus on God's mercy. As she grew in her awareness of God's mercy toward her, she wanted to share in his merciful love for the world. At one point, Jesus told her, "I desire that you make an offering of yourself for sinners and especially for those souls who have lost hope in God's mercy." So, as she prayed and went about her tasks in the convent, Faustina would mentally unite herself with Jesus in his offering of himself to God. She prayed especially on behalf of men and women who had turned away from God and lost hope of being welcomed back by him.

Faustina's diary is filled with notes recording moments when she felt Jesus speak to her about mercy. "My daughter, tell the whole world about My inconceivable mercy." "Everything that exists has come forth from the very depths of My most tender mercy." "Know, My daughter, that between Me and you there is a bottomless abyss, an abyss which separates the Creator from the creature. But this abyss is filled with My mercy." "Know that my heart is mercy itself. From this sea of mercy, graces flow out upon the whole world." "Let no one despair."

The keynote of response to God's mercy, Faustina emphasized, is trust in God. God calls us to trust in his presence and love whenever we find ourselves facing difficulties, sufferings, and misunderstandings by others, and especially when we experience our own sinfulness and weakness. Indeed, she said, God invites us to use our problems as an opportunity to participate in his mercy. Jesus told Faustina, "Join your sufferings to my passion and offer them to the heavenly Father for sinners."

Of course, sharing in God's mercy is not only a matter of praying but is something we express toward the people around us. Faustina wrote: "We resemble God most when we forgive our neighbors. God is Love, Goodness, and Mercy." Here she almost seems to be echoing God's words about himself in our Exodus reading: "The Lord, a God merciful and gracious, slow to anger, and abounding in steadfast love and faithfulness . . . forgiving iniquity and transgression and sin" (Exodus 34:6–7).

Faustina died of tuberculosis in 1938. In the years after her death, copies of the Divine Mercy image of Jesus began to circulate in Poland, along with reports of her revelations. But a poorly translated version of her diary created an unfavorable impression in the Vatican. In 1958, Church authorities prohibited any promotion of Faustina, her writings, or her picture of Jesus.

Faustina might have been headed for oblivion but for the interest of a Polish seminarian named Karol Wojtyla. During World War II, under the German occupation, he was forced to work at a chemical plant that happened to be within sight of the convent cemetery where Faustina was buried. Young Wojtyla found inspiration in Faustina's devotion to God's mercy. When he became the bishop of Krakow in the 1960s, he persuaded Vatican officials that they had misunderstood Faustina. He instituted the process for her recognition as a saint.

When Wojtyla became Pope John Paul II, he declared that his special task as pope was to deliver the message of God's mercy through Christ to the world. He promoted Faustina's revelations and writings as an authentic and timely reminder of this mercy. In 2000,

John Paul declared Faustina a saint and decreed that each year the first Sunday after Easter would be dedicated to Divine Mercy. The timing of the feast serves to underline the purpose of the events celebrated during Holy Week and Easter: through Jesus' death and resurrection, God's mercy reaches out to sinful men and women to lift us from our sins and draw us into his own life.

At the Mass at which Faustina was canonized, the pope concluded his homily with this prayer:

And you, Faustina, a gift of God to our time, a gift from the land of Poland to the whole Church, obtain for us an awareness of the depth of divine mercy; help us to have a living experience of it and to bear witness to it among our brothers and sisters. May your message of light and hope spread throughout the world, spurring sinners to conversion, calming rivalries and hatred and opening individuals and nations to the practice of brotherhood. Today, fixing our gaze with you on the face of the risen Christ, let us make our own your prayer of trusting abandonment and say with firm hope: *Christ Jesus, I trust in you!*

Week 2

GOOD TO GO

Questions to Begin

10 minutes
Use a question or two to get warmed up for the reading.

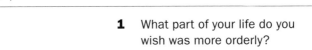

1   What part of your life do you
wish was more orderly?

2   To what older person have you
sometimes looked for advice?

I said to you, "Have no dread or fear of them. The LORD your
God . . . goes before you on the way to seek out a place for you
to camp, in fire by night, and in the cloud by day, to show you the
route you should take."

Deuteronomy 1:29–30, 33

Opening the Bible

10 minutes
Read the passage aloud. Let individuals take turns reading
paragraphs.

The Background

In the silence up on the heights of Mount Sinai, before the rude interruption of the golden bull, God had been giving Moses directions for constructing a "tabernacle," or tent shrine, for his presence among the Israelites. Now that the golden bull has been taken out of the way, work on the shrine can begin. In our first reading, Moses relays the directions to the people.

As the next reading begins, the shrine has been completed and God is giving further instructions, this time for the arrangement of the Israelites' camp. Our third and fourth readings describe two means by which God will guide the people once they leave Mount Sinai. The first means is surprising; the second, surprisingly ordinary.

The Reading: Exodus 35:4–21, 30–33; 36:1–3, 8; Numbers 2:1–3, 10, 17–18, 25, 34; 9:15–18, 21–22; 10:11–14, 29–34

The Shrine

Exodus 35:4 Moses said to all the congregation of the Israelites: This is the thing that the LORD has commanded: 5 Take from among you an offering to the LORD; let whoever is of a generous heart bring the LORD's offering: gold, silver, and bronze; 6 blue, purple, and crimson yarns, and fine linen; goats' hair, 7 tanned rams' skins, and fine leather; acacia wood, 8 oil for the light, spices for the anointing oil and for the fragrant incense, 9 and onyx stones and gems to be set in the ephod and the breastpiece.

10 All who are skillful among you shall come and make all that the LORD has commanded: the tabernacle, 11 its tent and its covering, its clasps and its frames, its bars, its pillars, and its bases; 12 the ark with its poles, the mercy seat, and the curtain for the screen; 13 the table with its poles and all its utensils, and the bread of the Presence; 14 the lampstand also for the light, with its utensils and its lamps, and the oil for the light; 15 and the altar of incense, with its poles, and the anointing oil and the fragrant incense, and

the screen for the entrance, the entrance of the tabernacle; 16 the
altar of burnt offering, with its grating of bronze, its poles, and all
its utensils, the basin with its stand; 17 the hangings of the court, its
pillars and its bases, and the screen for the gate of the court; 18 the
pegs of the tabernacle and the pegs of the court, and their cords;
19 the finely worked vestments for ministering in the holy place, the
holy vestments for the priest Aaron, and the vestments of his sons,
for their service as priests.

20 Then all the congregation of the Israelites withdrew from
the presence of Moses. 21 And they came, everyone whose heart
was stirred, and everyone whose spirit was willing, and brought the
Lord's offering to be used for the tent of meeting, and for all its
service, and for the sacred vestments. . . .

30 Then Moses said to the Israelites: See, the Lord has
called by name Bezalel son of Uri son of Hur, of the tribe of Judah;
31 he has filled him with divine spirit, with skill, intelligence, and
knowledge in every kind of craft, 32 to devise artistic designs, to
work in gold, silver, and bronze, 33 in cutting stones for setting,
and in carving wood, in every kind of craft. . . . 36:1 Bezalel and
Oholiab and every skillful one to whom the Lord has given skill and
understanding to know how to do any work in the construction of
the sanctuary shall work in accordance with all that the Lord has
commanded.

2 Moses then called Bezalel and Oholiab and every skillful one
to whom the Lord had given skill, everyone whose heart was stirred
to come to do the work; 3 and they received from Moses all the
freewill offerings that the Israelites had brought for doing the work
on the sanctuary. . . .

8 All those with skill among the workers made the
tabernacle. . . .

The Camp

Numbers 2:1 The Lord spoke to Moses and Aaron, saying: 2 The
Israelites shall camp each in their respective regiments, under
ensigns by their ancestral houses; they shall camp facing the tent
of meeting on every side. 3 Those to camp on the east side toward
the sunrise shall be of the regimental encampment of Judah by

companies. The leader of the people of Judah shall be Nahshon son of Amminadab. . . .

10 On the south side shall be the regimental encampment of Reuben by companies. The leader of the Reubenites shall be Elizur son of Shedeur. . . .

17 The tent of meeting, with the camp of the Levites, shall set out in the center of the camps; they shall set out just as they camp, each in position, by their regiments.

18 On the west side shall be the regimental encampment of Ephraim by companies. The leader of the people of Ephraim shall be Elishama son of Ammihud. . . .

25 On the north side shall be the regimental encampment of Dan by companies. The leader of the Danites shall be Ahiezer son of Ammishaddai. . . .

34 The Israelites did just as the LORD had commanded Moses: They camped by regiments, and they set out the same way, everyone by clans, according to ancestral houses.

The Cloud

9:15 On the day the tabernacle was set up, the cloud covered the tabernacle, the tent of the covenant; and from evening until morning it was over the tabernacle, having the appearance of fire. 16 It was always so: the cloud covered it by day and the appearance of fire by night.

17 Whenever the cloud lifted from over the tent, then the Israelites would set out; and in the place where the cloud settled down, there the Israelites would camp. 18 At the command of the LORD the Israelites would set out, and at the command of the LORD they would camp. As long as the cloud rested over the tabernacle, they would remain in camp. . . .

21 Sometimes the cloud would remain from evening until morning; and when the cloud lifted in the morning, they would set out, or if it continued for a day and a night, when the cloud lifted they would set out. 22 Whether it was two days, or a month, or a longer time, that the cloud continued over the tabernacle, resting upon it, the Israelites would remain in camp and would not set out; but when it lifted they would set out. . . .

10:11 In the second year, in the second month, on the twentieth day of the month, the cloud lifted from over the tabernacle of the covenant. 12 Then the Israelites set out by stages from the wilderness of Sinai, and the cloud settled down in the wilderness of Paran. 13 They set out for the first time at the command of the LORD by Moses. 14 The standard of the camp of Judah set out first, company by company. . . .

The Father-in-Law

29 Moses said to Hobab son of Reuel the Midianite, Moses' father-in-law, "We are setting out for the place of which the LORD said, 'I will give it to you'; come with us, and we will treat you well; for the LORD has promised good to Israel." 30 But he said to him, "I will not go, but I will go back to my own land and to my kindred." 31 He said, "Do not leave us, for you know where we should camp in the wilderness, and you will serve as eyes for us. 32 Moreover, if you go with us, whatever good the LORD does for us, the same we will do for you."

33 So they set out from the mount of the LORD three days' journey with the ark of the covenant of the LORD going before them three days' journey, to seek out a resting place for them, 34 the cloud of the LORD being over them by day when they set out from the camp.

First Impression

5 minutes
Briefly mention a question you have about the reading or one thing in it that surprised, impressed, delighted, or challenged you. No discussion! Just listen to one another's reactions.

Exploring the Theme

If participants have not read this section already, read it aloud.
Otherwise go on to "Questions for Reflection and Discussion."

Exodus 35–36. God gave Moses such elaborate plans for the tent shrine and its equipment that the details fill seven biblical chapters (Exodus 25–31). In our first reading, we see the Israelites beginning to act on these directions. The account of the construction extends from chapter 35 to chapter 40 of Exodus and mostly follows the earlier directions word for word. This point-by-point repetition shows that the Israelites do *precisely* what God has told them to do (it also makes these chapters ideal for insomniacs). The Israelites are making good use of the second chance God has given them.

God forbade images like the bull statue in order to help the Israelites realize that he transcends his creation. The universe contains nothing that can adequately symbolize the infinitely wise, powerful, good creator. He surpasses every human conception. Through the tent shrine, however, God balances this truth with another: while he is transcendent, he is not distant. God lives among us. No artificial mechanisms, such as bull statues, are needed to secure his presence. God comes among us not because we figure out how to conjure him up but because he wants to be with us. He is God in our midst—as one of his biblical titles "Immanuel" declares ("Immanuel"—Isaiah 7:14—is Hebrew for "God is with us"). His coming among us will reach a climax in his actually becoming one of us, sharing our humanity, in Jesus of Nazareth (Matthew 1:23; John 1:1–18).

There isn't enough space here to explore the tabernacle and its furnishings in detail (a study Bible will help you do that; see page 96). Briefly, however, the "ephod" (35:9) is a vestment worn by the high priest. The "ark" (35:12) is a wooden chest in which the stone tablets of the law (Exodus 34:28) are kept. The ark is the central object within the tabernacle. The "mercy seat" (35:12) is the ark's carved lid.

The tabernacle is composed of various materials, some rare and expensive, and various skills are required to fashion them into the finished product. This gives many people a chance to make a contribution by donating materials and using their skills. Do skills such as metalworking and embroidery seem unspiritual? The reading indicates that they are gifts from God. Consider Bezalel: the Lord "has filled him with divine spirit, with skill, intelligence, and knowledge in every kind of craft" (35:31). Thus, God inspires not only Moses to teach and Aaron to minister as a priest but also Bezalel and Oholiab and those who work under their direction to produce beautiful objects with precious metals, fabrics, and wood.

Notice the emphasis on freedom. God so values each person's offering that there must be no coercion or pressure on the givers, for that would destroy their opportunity to respond freely to his invitation.

Numbers 2. Again, we can't go into the details concerning the layout of the tent shrine and the camp. What is important here is simply to get the basic idea of the arrangement. The tent shrine is a rectangle, and the people camp by tribes in rectangular formation around it, "facing the tent of meeting on every side" (2:2). Situated at the center of the camp, the shrine is a visual reminder that God expects to be the center of all the Israelites' activities and relationships. Because he dwells at the center of their community, the Israelites' primary activity is worship—a subject that is developed at length in Exodus, Leviticus, Numbers, and Deuteronomy (see, for example, Leviticus chapters 1–7, 16, 21–25, 27). In last week's reading, God's presence was seen to be dangerous for those who reject his commands. The present reading brings out a complementary truth: for those who cooperate with him, God's presence is the source of order and harmony.

Some of the terminology—"regiments" (2:2) and "companies" (2:3)—is distinctly military. The people are civilians, not professional soldiers, but they are organized like troops mustered for action. This is a way of expressing their submission to God's authority. It is also a preparation for conflicts ahead. As we will see, people along the Israelites' route will try to block their progress to the land God wishes to give them.

Verse 17 describes how the Israelites will proceed when they depart from Mount Sinai. Just as the members of the tribe of Levi set their tents in the middle of the camp near the tabernacle, so they will be in the middle of the line of march, carrying the tent and its equipment.

Our reading gives us a picture of the Israelites neatly lined up, like high school seniors sitting for a class photo. We may wonder whether this external order reflects an inner submission to God's will. Not long before, these same people were whooping it up in front of a golden bull. Are they now as *truly* devoted to God as they seem to express by the orderly arrangement of their tents around his shrine?

Numbers 9:15–10:14. The author continues to describe how things will proceed when the Israelites get under way. God will guide them by means of a column of fire wrapped in cloud. By day, in the sunlight, only the cloud can be seen. But at night the fire becomes visible—an awesome sight, we can be sure. The fiery cloud will move forward and stop, indicating when and where the Israelites are to go and when and where they are to camp. Like the preceding reading, this one gives us a picture of the Israelites as a compact group, harmoniously following God's directions.

The simple fact that God's shrine is in the form of a tent is worth pondering. Unlike a stone temple, this sanctuary can be moved. The portable shrine symbolizes a mobile God. The God of Israel is present with his people wherever they go. Unlike the Egyptian and Canaanite gods, he is not especially identified with any particular land. No place in the world is farther from him than any other. He is close to us when we turn to him, no matter where.

Numbers 10:29–34. At long last, the day of departure has arrived. The Israelites have been camping at Mount Sinai for almost a year. Now they literally pull up stakes and move on. Things go well. Everyone proceeds according to God's plan (10:13–14).

The fiery cloud powerfully signifies that the initiative lies with God. He determines where the people should go. Their task is not to decide which direction to take but to pay attention to the direction in which God is leading them.

Given the emphasis on God's guidance, the final incident in our readings comes as something of a surprise (10:29–34). If the Israelites have the guidance of the cloud, why would they need Moses' father-in-law Hobab to show them where to camp (10:31)?

The biblical author does not answer the question. But by setting Moses' conversation with Hobab after the description of the fiery cloud, the author seems to suggest that while God sometimes guides us through extraordinary means, normal means of discovering his will retain their importance. Experience and study, thinking and consulting, learning by trial and error—all play a part in discovering what God is calling us to do. In the end, it makes no difference whether God guides us through ordinary or extraordinary means. What matters is our seeking his will and doing it.

Moses is insistent that Hobab accompany the Israelites (10:31–32). Biblical scholar Dennis T. Olson remarks that Moses "will not easily take 'no' for an answer, even from God (Exodus 32:10–14; 33:17)!" Although the author does not say so here, apparently Moses succeeds in persuading Hobab to accept his invitation, for Hobab's descendants are later mentioned as living in Canaan with the Israelites (Judges 1:16; 4:11). Moses' invitation to Hobab to share in Israel's covenant with God may be representative of what happened with the Israelites' neighbors on a larger scale than the Old Testament indicates. Neighboring peoples may have been invited to join in the covenant between God and Israel.

Our readings offer thought-provoking images that we may apply to the life of the Church. The Church, too, is to be a community in which all are attentive to God's presence at the center of life. Now that Jesus has replaced the tabernacle as the perfect focal point of God's presence among us, the picture of the Israelites camped around the tabernacle may serve as a visual expression of the ideal for Jesus' disciples: to be gathered around him, attentive to the order and harmony he wishes to give us. Like the tabernacle, Jesus also is moving on—seeking to find entry in all nations, cultures, organizations, and families. He invites us to move on with him, guided by his Spirit.

Questions for Reflection and Discussion

45 minutes
Choose questions according to your interest and time.

1 The Israelites' tent shrine would have been beautiful. What difference does it make if the place for worshiping God is beautiful? Is it possible to put too much emphasis on making worship beautiful? What makes worship truly beautiful?

2 Moses' reference to generous giving (Exodus 35:5) harmonizes with St. Paul's statement that "God loves a cheerful giver" (2 Corinthians 9:7). When have you given cheerfully? grudgingly? Do you need improvement in this area?

3 What makes talents, skills, and resources spiritual? What talents do you possess? Are they spiritual? What does it mean for you to use them in a spiritual way? Do you?

4 God gave the Israelites a second chance when he forgave them for making the golden bull. When have you had a second chance? How well did you make use of it? What role can the sacrament of Reconciliation play in this process? Is God giving you a second chance now in some area of your life?

5 What helps you to perceive the hidden reality of God's presence in the Church? in yourself? in your relationships with other people? What reminds you of God's presence? How could you make more use of this reminder?

6 How could you contribute to greater order and harmony in some situation in which you are regularly involved?

7 Identify an area in which the Church needs guidance today. How does God guide the Church in regard to matters such as this? How can laypeople contribute to the Church's being able to discern God's will? What contribution can you make?

8 **Focus question.** How have you experienced God's guidance in your personal life? What have you learned about discerning God's will? Are there people whose wisdom you have learned to value in discerning God's will? What qualities make them wise? How could you learn more from them? Where in your life do you feel a need for God's guidance and wisdom? What could you do to find what you need?

Prayer to Close

10 minutes
Use this approach—or create your own!

◆ Call on the Holy Spirit to be with you. Then take a few minutes for silent reflection. Consider the gifts and talents God has given you and how you are using them. Ask for the openness and courage to welcome new gifts and place them at God's disposal. Close by praying together an Our Father or this prayer:

Lord, we place ourselves before you. We offer you all that we are and all that we have. Receive our resources, gifts, talents, abilities—those we recognize and those we don't. Forgive us for all the times we've held back from using them in your service.
    Stir our hearts to serve you cheerfully. Sustain in us a willing Spirit. Help us to work together for the building of your Church, the well-being of our neighbors, the coming of your kingdom. Amen.

Saints in the Making

A Beckoning Image

Catholic writer Antoinette Bosco describes a shopping expedition as a teen with her mother. Walking down the street, Bosco unexpectedly had a mental image of Jesus. He was "pouring out love from his Sacred Heart," she writes. "He was in profile, looking down, with his right hand extended in welcome. But it was his left hand that drew me, beckoning me to come to him." A minute later Bosco walked past a religious goods store and was astonished to see in the window a framed version of the image that had just flashed into her mind. "From high up on that wall, it was as if Jesus was looking down at me, clearly beckoning me. I was mesmerized." She went in the store, made a fifty-cent deposit on the picture, and returned soon to pay the remaining two dollars of the purchase price. Her account of the picture continues:

I remember how I hugged it as I carried it home, and hung it on a nail on the wall in my bedroom. I would think sometimes of how strange it had been that I had actually "seen" this image of Jesus before it was humanly possible to have really seen it, or to know that it was in the religious goods store. In my youthful way, I took this as a sign that Jesus was calling me, that he beckoned to me because I was special, good, and holy.

Ah, how nice it is to be young, untried, unwounded by life, sure of yourself, sure of your strength, and still protected from having to drink of the chalice in the garden of Gethsemane. I was, rather soon, to learn a different lesson from my gift of the image. It had been given to me not because I was deserving of a special grace, but because I would need a special grace to survive my life without despair. And that special grace was to be able to look at that image of Jesus, being constantly reminded that he was beckoning me, assuring me that no matter what I was going through in my life, he would be there to hold me with his extended right hand as he never stopped beckoning to me with his left. All I had to do was believe him and follow him.

That plaque of Jesus has been on my wall next to my bed for nearly sixty years, through twelve moves from towns and cities as I completed my education during wartime, married and raised a family, endured a divorce, and faced the tragic deaths of two sons, a daughter-in-law, and so many loved ones. I never ever saw another plaque, or even a drawing, like this one. It was, and is, a gift, but it came with a challenge. That hand of Jesus, beckoning me, raised valid questions. Who would I be following? Who is this Jesus who wants me to take his hand? Who would I become if I trusted him so surely? And did he hold his hand out to others as powerfully as he did to me? Bottom line—he caught my attention in a way that cannot be explained scientifically, but catch it he did, permanently.

The unusual way that Bosco discovered the picture of Jesus sets her experience apart from that of most of us. But treasuring a particular image of the Lord is probably fairly common. The Gospels do not give us a physical description of Jesus, and no artist painted a portrait of him during his lifetime, so we do not know what he actually looked like. But this has given artists freedom to depict him in a wide variety of ways. Each artist communicates the impression that Jesus has made on him or her. From the various depictions, many of us find one that is especially helpful in reflecting who Jesus is for us.

The Israelites had a mysterious cloud as an expression of God's presence and guidance, but his personal call to us has now become incarnate in Jesus of Nazareth. Jesus invites each of us to follow him on the particular path through life that God has created for us to travel. Like Antoinette Bosco, many of us have found that an image of Jesus can be a challenging and comforting reminder of his presence with us on the way. Has this been your experience? If so, how might you give this image a more prominent place in your prayer? If not, have you thought of searching for a portrayal of Jesus that speaks to you?

THIS WAY IS HARD!

Questions to Begin

10 minutes
Use a question or two to get warmed up for the reading.

1 What do you like most about traveling? least?

2 What's the hardest trip you ever took?

3 Were you ever sorry that you got something you had wished for? ever happy that you did not get something you had wished for?

We must not put Christ to the test, as some of them did, and were destroyed by serpents.

1 Corinthians 10:9

Opening the Bible

10 minutes
Read the passage aloud. Let individuals take turns reading
paragraphs.

The Background

No sooner have the Israelites set out from Mount Sinai—a mere
two verses after our last reading in Week 2—than they begin to
complain. No doubt they face privations in the wilderness. In fact,
they have serious needs, beginning with water and food. But God
has shown his commitment to care for them (Exodus 15:22–16:36),
miraculously providing water and a food called *manna* that mysteri-
ously appears on the ground each morning. We may wonder why the
people can't tough it out and show a little trust in God.

   Our second, third, and fourth readings come from later
stages in the Israelites' journey—demonstrating that their griping
was not a onetime phenomenon.

The Reading: Numbers 11:1–16, 18–23, 31–34; 20:1–13; 21:4–9

Complaining

11:1 Now when the people complained in the hearing of the LORD
about their misfortunes, the LORD heard it and his anger was
kindled. Then the fire of the LORD burned against them, and
consumed some outlying parts of the camp. 2 But the people cried
out to Moses; and Moses prayed to the LORD, and the fire abated.
3 So that place was called Taberah,* because the fire of the LORD
burned against them.

Complaining

4 The rabble among them had a strong craving; and the Israelites also
wept again, and said, "If only we had meat to eat! 5 We remember
the fish we used to eat in Egypt for nothing, the cucumbers, the
melons, the leeks, the onions, and the garlic; 6 but now our strength
is dried up, and there is nothing at all but this manna to look at."

*That is *Burning*

7 Now the manna was like coriander seed, and its color was like the color of gum resin. 8 The people went around and gathered it, ground it in mills or beat it in mortars, then boiled it in pots and made cakes of it; and the taste of it was like the taste of cakes baked with oil. 9 When the dew fell on the camp in the night, the manna would fall with it.

10 Moses heard the people weeping throughout their families, all at the entrances of their tents. Then the LORD became very angry, and Moses was displeased. 11 So Moses said to the LORD, "Why have you treated your servant so badly? Why have I not found favor in your sight, that you lay the burden of all this people on me? 12 Did I conceive all this people? Did I give birth to them, that you should say to me, 'Carry them in your bosom, as a nurse carries a sucking child,' to the land that you promised on oath to their ancestors? 13 Where am I to get meat to give to all this people? For they come weeping to me and say, 'Give us meat to eat!' 14 I am not able to carry all this people alone, for they are too heavy for me. 15 If this is the way you are going to treat me, put me to death at once—if I have found favor in your sight—and do not let me see my misery."

16 So the LORD said to Moses, . . . 18 ". . . say to the people: Consecrate yourselves for tomorrow, and you shall eat meat; for you have wailed in the hearing of the LORD, saying, 'If only we had meat to eat! Surely it was better for us in Egypt.' Therefore the LORD will give you meat, and you shall eat. 19 You shall eat not only one day, or two days, or five days, or ten days, or twenty days, 20 but for a whole month—until it comes out of your nostrils and becomes loathsome to you—because you have rejected the LORD who is among you, and have wailed before him, saying, 'Why did we ever leave Egypt?'"

21 But Moses said, "The people I am with number six hundred thousand on foot; and you say, 'I will give them meat, that they may eat for a whole month'! 22 Are there enough flocks and herds to slaughter for them? Are there enough fish in the sea to catch for them?"

23 The LORD said to Moses, "Is the LORD's power limited? Now you shall see whether my word will come true for you or not." . . .

31 Then a wind went out from the LORD, and it brought quails from the sea and let them fall beside the camp, about a day's journey on this side and a day's journey on the other side, all around the camp, about two cubits deep on the ground. 32 So the people worked all that day and night and all the next day, gathering the quails; the least anyone gathered was ten homers; and they spread them out for themselves all around the camp. 33 But while the meat was still between their teeth, before it was consumed, the anger of the LORD was kindled against the people, and the LORD struck the people with a very great plague. 34 So that place was called Kibroth-hattaavah,* because there they buried the people who had the craving.

Complaining

20:1 The Israelites, the whole congregation, came into the wilderness of Zin in the first month, and the people stayed in Kadesh. . . .

2 Now there was no water for the congregation; so they gathered together against Moses and against Aaron. 3 The people quarreled with Moses and said, "Would that we had died when our kindred died before the LORD! 4 Why have you brought the assembly of the LORD into this wilderness for us and our livestock to die here? 5 Why have you brought us up out of Egypt, to bring us to this wretched place? It is no place for grain, or figs, or vines, or pomegranates; and there is no water to drink."

6 Then Moses and Aaron went away from the assembly to the entrance of the tent of meeting; they fell on their faces, and the glory of the LORD appeared to them. 7 The LORD spoke to Moses, saying: 8 Take the staff, and assemble the congregation, you and your brother Aaron, and command the rock before their eyes to yield its water. Thus you shall bring water out of the rock for them; thus you shall provide drink for the congregation and their livestock.

9 So Moses took the staff from before the LORD, as he had commanded him. 10 Moses and Aaron gathered the assembly together before the rock, and he said to them, "Listen, you rebels, shall we bring water for you out of this rock?" 11 Then Moses lifted up his hand and struck the rock twice with his staff; water came out abundantly, and the congregation and their livestock drank.

*That is *Graves of craving*

12 But the LORD said to Moses and Aaron, "Because you did not trust in me, to show my holiness before the eyes of the Israelites, therefore you shall not bring this assembly into the land that I have given them."

13 These are the waters of Meribah,* where the people of Israel quarreled with the LORD, and by which he showed his holiness.

Still Complaining

21:4 From Mount Hor they set out by the way to the Red Sea, to go around the land of Edom; but the people became impatient on the way. 5 The people spoke against God and against Moses, "Why have you brought us up out of Egypt to die in the wilderness? For there is no food and no water, and we detest this miserable food." 6 Then the LORD sent poisonous serpents among the people, and they bit the people, so that many Israelites died.

7 The people came to Moses and said, "We have sinned by speaking against the LORD and against you; pray to the LORD to take away the serpents from us." So Moses prayed for the people.

8 And the LORD said to Moses, "Make a poisonous serpent, and set it on a pole; and everyone who is bitten shall look at it and live." 9 So Moses made a serpent of bronze, and put it upon a pole; and whenever a serpent bit someone, that person would look at the serpent of bronze and live.

*That is *Quarrel*

First Impression

5 minutes
Briefly mention a question you have about the reading or one thing in it that surprised, impressed, delighted, or challenged you. No discussion! Just listen to one another's reactions.

Exploring the Theme

If participants have not read this section already, read it aloud.
Otherwise go on to "Questions for Reflection and Discussion."

11:1–3. It is easy to understand why the Israelites complain. The
Sinai Peninsula is hard going. Yet the people's rebellion is a bit
surprising. It seems like only yesterday they were marshaled as a
well-ordered army, following God's instructions to the letter. Their
unexpected rejection of God's purposes may remind us of Adam and
Eve in the garden of Eden (Genesis 3). There, too, the abandonment
of God's way came out of the blue. In neither case does the author
seem to supply a completely adequate explanation for these acts
of rebellion—perhaps suggesting that there is something illogical
about rejecting God's plans for us.

11:4–34. The "rabble" (Numbers 11:4) may be non-
Israelites who joined the Israelites when they escaped from Egypt
(Exodus 12:38). They do not lack what they need. They are simply
bored with their diet (Numbers 11:4–6). The manna keeps them
alive, but they would prefer fresh fish and crispy salads. In the
Hebrew text, they declare literally that their "gullets are withered"
from the manna (Numbers 11:6). The author makes it clear that
their perception is distorted (Numbers 11:7–9). Nothing about the
manna would dry out the throat. It cooks up into an olive-oil flavored
cake that would gain the accolade every baker hopes to hear: "Why,
it's so moist!"

The complainers are suffering from selective memory
loss. Granted, in Egypt they ate "for nothing" (Numbers 11:5): as
slaves, they were fed, perhaps fed well. But their life was bitter
(Exodus 1:13–14; 2:23). Now they have freedom, but they are not
willing to endure the hardships that come with it. Instead of taking
responsibility for responding to God's call to them, they act like
children who blame others if things don't go their way.

So far, Moses has played the role of adult for the
group—and he's getting tired of it. Feeling pressure from both the
people and God, his perception—like that of the Israelites—also is
distorted. His complaint to God about the Israelites—"They come
weeping to me and say, 'Give us meat to eat!'" (Numbers 11:13)—
seems exaggerated (compare Numbers 11:4 and 11:10). To judge
from his testy reply to God's promise of meat—"Are there enough

flocks and herds to slaughter for them?" (Numbers 11:22)—Moses feels that God expects *him* to provide meat for the people; yet God has placed no such requirement on him.

Moses has been displeased, even angry, with the people before (Exodus 32:17–20); but now he seems totally exasperated with them. He is also unhappy with God for saddling him with responsibility for them. Stuck between whining people and (as he sees it) a demanding God, Moses gives way to self-pity. His earlier concern for the people is replaced with self-concern. At Mount Sinai he stood *with* the people in order to persuade God to be merciful to them; now he distances himself from them. Instead of using his special relationship with God as a basis for appealing on their behalf ("If I have found favor in your sight . . . consider . . . that this nation is your people"—Exodus 33:13), he uses his special relationship with God to appeal to be rid of them ("Put me to death at once—if I have found favor in your sight"—Numbers 11:15).

God is the only one whose perceptions remain realistic (Numbers 11:16–23). He carefully distinguishes between the complaint of the people and Moses' complaint. God interprets the people's complaint as an expression of rebellion, deserving punishment. But he deals patiently with Moses, apparently taking Moses' complaint as a sign of exhaustion. Significantly, Moses brings his dissatisfaction directly to God; the Israelites merely weep by their tents (11:10–11). In his distress Moses, like the psalmists, struggles with God; the Israelites ignore God.

Perhaps the Israelites do not address their concerns to God because they are unwilling to obey him. Their assertion that "surely it was better for us in Egypt" (Numbers 11:18) is a rejection of God's plan for them and thus a rejection of God himself (see Numbers 11:20). Their complaint implies that they were better off before they started relating to God. Apparently they know better than God what is good for them. Here, again, they may remind us of Adam and Eve—and of ourselves?

The quail come in immense quantities, piling up a yard deep on the ground ("two cubits"—Numbers 11:31). Each person gathers up at least "ten homers" (Numbers 11:32), that is, ten donkey loads (*homer* is related to the Hebrew word for

donkey)—equivalent to more than ten fifty-five-gallon drums.
Yet, unlike the water and manna, the quail are more curse than
blessing. Significantly, the quail do not fall *in* the camp, where
God is especially present in the tabernacle, but "beside" the camp
(Numbers 11:31), that is, outside of it. The blessings of material
abundance become the opposite of a blessing to those who reject
God's will.

Apparently with this incident in mind, Paul wrote that "these
things occurred as examples for us, so that we might not desire evil
as they did" (1 Corinthians 10:6). Paul seems particularly to mean
that the Israelites' experience was a warning against an excessive
desire even for things that are naturally good.

20:1–13. This time the Israelites have a genuine need.
They are out of water (Numbers 20:2). Rather than praying for
God's help, however, they complain to Moses. And, as before, they
repudiate God's plan for them: they do not berate Moses for taking
the wrong path in the wilderness but for leading them out of Egypt in
the first place (Numbers 20:5). They continue to look back fondly to
Egypt, forgetting that, for them, Egypt had hardly been a resort.

Fearing that a terrible disaster will follow this further
expression of rebellion against God, Moses and Aaron prostrate
themselves before God in a plea for leniency (20:6). God, however,
displays no anger toward the people. He simply gives Moses
directions for how to get water. Moses should take the staff that
is kept in the tabernacle and command "the rock"—apparently a
nearby cliff or massive boulder—to give water (Numbers 20:8).

In what follows, the most surprising element is not the
flow of water from a solid rock—marvels of this kind have already
occurred on this miracle-studded journey—but God's rebuke of
Moses and Aaron (Numbers 20:12). What exactly is their sin?
Various explanations are possible (see page 58). In any case, God
declares, "You did not trust in me" (Numbers 20:12), and for this
he bars them from the land he is planning to give the people. This is
severe, but God is not holding the two leaders to a higher standard
than everyone else. The same requirement applies to all: to obtain
God's promises, you must trust him.

In this episode, Moses and Aaron treat the people with anger and disdain ("you rebels"—Numbers 20:10), while God provides what the people need without addressing their bad attitude. He acts like a parent who always provides what the children need without trying to correct every fault.

21:4–9. The Israelites complain "on the way" (21:4). The Hebrew could be translated "because of the journey," and the journey certainly gives ample cause for unhappiness. The Israelites have to make a detour around a territory called Edom that takes them into southwestern Jordan, which is very hot! Unlike previous occasions of complaining, the people direct their complaint not only to Moses but also to God (Numbers 21:5; compare 11:1; 11:4; 20:3–4). Although they have a real need, they are, in addition, totally out of patience and are not making too much sense, as you can see from a careful reading of verse 5. When poisonous snakes attack them, they have something more serious to be concerned about. But this time, instead of grumbling disrespectfully, they make a humble plea to Moses to ask God to help them (21:7).

The bronze snake that Moses makes seems almost magical (21:8–9). But it is not a tool by which people can get God to do what they want. Nor does it have any power of its own. The metal snake brings healing only because God works through it. As a visible means by which God heals, it might be compared to the mud that Jesus occasionally uses in the process of healing (John 9:6–15). Indeed, the bronze snake functions as an invitation to faith in God, because looking at the snake is a way for an afflicted person to express their appeal to God. It may be worth noting that, unlike the golden bull statue that the Israelites made earlier (Exodus 32), the bronze snake is not intended as an image of God but is simply an instrument through which God chooses to act.

Jesus will compare himself to this bronze snake. Just as the snake was lifted up and all who looked at it were healed, Jesus will be lifted up in crucifixion and resurrection for the eternal healing of all who believe in him (John 3:16–17).

Questions for Reflection and Discussion

45 minutes
Choose questions according to your interest and time.

1 Compare Moses in these readings and in the readings in Weeks 1 and 2. Is Moses changing?

2 Compare Moses' account in Numbers 11:13 with the author's account in verses 4 and 10. How is Moses' report different from the author's? What does this suggest about Moses?

3 Reread Numbers 11:23. When have you experienced God's word coming true for you?

4 In what situations in your life have you acted like the Israelites in any of this week's readings? What was the result?

5 When have you acted like Moses in any of these readings?

6 When has your life seemed like a journey through a wilderness? What has been the manna through which God has kept you going? When have you experienced God unexpectedly giving you what you needed for your journey through life?

7 When have difficulties and stress made it hard for you to keep a balanced perspective on your situation? What have you learned from this experience?

8 Is all complaining rebellion against God? Are there better and worse ways to tell God about our problems? good and bad ways of complaining?

9 How can a person distinguish their needs from their wants?

10 Have you ever thought that your life might have been easier if you had not been a Christian? Would it have been *better*?

11 For Personal Reflection: When do you complain? What do you complain about? Who do you complain to? Does it do any good? any harm? What else could you do about the problem? What does your complaining tell you about yourself? about your relationship with God?

12 **Focus question.** Are the Israelites slow to learn that God is on their side when they face difficulties? How does trust in God grow? What has helped you grow in trust of God? Is there a decision involved?

Prayer to Close

10 minutes
Use this approach—or create your own!

◆ An antidote to complaining is the habit of thanking God. Have someone read the following reflections:

Every joy and suffering, every event and need can become the matter for thanksgiving which, sharing in that of Christ, should fill one's whole life: "Give thanks in all circumstances" (1 Thessalonians 5:18).
   Catechism of the Catholic Church, section 2648

Value the least gift as much as the greatest, the simplest as much as the most special. If you consider the dignity of the Giver, no gift will appear too small or worthless.
   Thomas à Kempis, *The Imitation of Christ*

Pause for silent reflection, then close with an Our Father.

Between Discussions

Moses' Sin

The episode at Meribah, in which Moses brings water out of a rock, is one of the most puzzling in the Bible. Moses, a towering and exemplary figure, makes a single mistake—and God instantly shuts him out of the promised land. Why does God impose such a severe penalty for a minor failure? Why doesn't God cut his long-suffering servant a little slack? Or is Moses' offense more serious than it appears? This brings us to the heart of the puzzle. What *is* Moses' sin?

Here again is the account in Numbers 20. What answer to the question can you find in it?

7 The LORD spoke to Moses, saying: 8 Take the staff, and assemble the congregation, you and your brother Aaron, and command the rock before their eyes to yield its water. Thus you shall bring water out of the rock for them; thus you shall provide drink for the congregation and their livestock.

9 So Moses took the staff from before the LORD, as he had commanded him. 10 Moses and Aaron gathered the assembly together before the rock, and he said to them, "Listen, you rebels, shall we bring water for you out of this rock?" 11 Then Moses lifted up his hand and struck the rock twice with his staff; water came out abundantly, and the congregation and their livestock drank.

12 But the LORD said to Moses and Aaron, "Because you did not trust in me, to show my holiness before the eyes of the Israelites, therefore you shall not bring this assembly into the land that I have given them."

Over the centuries, three main explanations of Moses' sin have been proposed (Aaron is also held guilty, but Moses is the key player).

1. *Moses casts doubt on God's power.*

This explanation focuses on the first part of God's verdict: "Because you did not trust in me" (Numbers 20:12).

Like all three explanations, this one involves a certain way of hearing Moses' words: "Listen, you rebels, shall we bring water for you out of this rock?" (Numbers 20:10). This could be taken as a temptation to doubt. Moses' question might be paraphrased: "Do you *really* believe we can bring water out of this rock? Do you believe God can do it?" The expected answer is, "Of course not. Nobody can bring water out of the face of a cliff."

Moses' action with the staff may lend support to the view that Moses' faith is weak. God instructs Moses to bring the staff but does not tell him to use it; Moses is to command the rock to give water. Perhaps Moses hits the rock with his staff because he is afraid that water will not come out of the rock if he simply speaks to it. Further evidence for this explanation: Moses strikes the rock twice. Perhaps he strikes the rock once and waits; when no water comes out, fearing that nothing will happen, he strikes the rock again.

Moses expressed doubt about God's ability to perform wonders on an earlier occasion, when the people demanded meat (Numbers 11:21–22). So it is easy to believe that he might doubt God's power in the present episode. This line of reasoning, however, leads to a further question. If God did not punish Moses for his doubts in the earlier episode, why would he punish him for lack of faith now? A possible answer is that earlier, Moses expressed his doubts to God directly, whereas now he displays his doubts in front of the people. Jewish scholar Jacob Milgrom relates a rabbinic story in which God discusses these two incidents with Moses and explains why he is going to deal with Moses more severely now. "The first offense that you committed was a private matter between you and Me," God says. "Now, however, that it is done in the presence of the public it is impossible to overlook."

2. *Moses fails to reflect God's compassion.*

This explanation gives a certain interpretation of God's words to Moses, "you did not trust in me, to *show my holiness* before the eyes of the Israelites" (Numbers 20:12, emphasis added). According to this explanation, Moses would have showed God's holiness if he had reflected God's compassion.

Instead, Moses expressed bitterness, which did not manifest God's holiness at all.

This explanation detects a note of contempt in Moses' words to the people. "Listen, you rebels, shall we bring water for you out of this rock?" (Numbers 20:10) sounds like a taunt: "Shall we bring water out of the rock for you? Let's hear you beg for it, you creeps!" Or his words may sound as though he is toying with them: "You rebels! Why should we give *you* water? Sure, we could bring water out of the rock. But do you think we'll do it for the likes of you? Forget it!" Moses could even be understood as making a veiled threat: "You rebels, don't you remember the quail? When you whined about the lack of meat, God crammed you with so much meat you got sick. Now do you want us to bring water out of the rock—and drown the lot of you?"

It is easy to picture Moses being angry in this episode. The people are behaving badly. Perhaps more upsetting to Moses, God does not rebuke them. So perhaps Moses takes it upon himself to make up for this "defect" in God's response.

The possibility that Moses' sin is anger finds support in a reference to the incident in one of the psalms. The psalmist writes that the people angered God at the waters of Meribah, "and it went ill with Moses on their account; for they made his spirit bitter, and he spoke words that were rash" (Psalm 106:32–33). This suggests that the people provoked Moses to anger, and God held him accountable for his angry words.

3. *Moses leads the people to think that he possesses magical powers.*

This explanation focuses especially on one word in God's verdict: "Because you did not trust in me, to show *my* holiness before the eyes of the Israelites" (Numbers 20:12, emphasis added). Instead of clearly attributing the miracle to God's power—according to this explanation—Moses conducts himself in a way that implies that he himself possesses wonder-working powers. Thus Moses, rather than God, gains honor from the miracle.

As with the other explanations, this one also detects a particular tone in Moses' words. "Listen, you rebels, shall *we* bring water for you out of this rock?" (Numbers 20:10, emphasis added). In other words, "Do you believe *we* can do it?" Ah, the little word *we*—"the fatal pronoun," Milgrom calls it.

How is this interpretation supported in the account? Moses' striking the rock—which he was not told to do—could have been viewed by the people as a magical act. Moses might have looked like a wizard with a magic wand, rather than a humble servant of the all-powerful God.

So what conclusion can we reach about Moses' sin? Do any of these explanations seem persuasive to you? It seems to me that there is evidence to support all the explanations offered here, but not enough evidence to show that one explanation should be accepted while the others should be ruled out. We seem to be unable to give a final answer to the question: What was Moses' sin?

This is puzzling. Why would the Bible raise such an important question while seemingly making it impossible to reach a definitive answer? St. Augustine remarked that there is a lot to be gained from wrestling with the difficulties of Scripture, even when we cannot resolve them. In this case, trying to understand Moses' sin leads us to read and reread the biblical text carefully—always a useful thing to do. Our search here has led us to reflect on the importance of trusting God, of expressing his compassion, of bearing with other people's failings patiently, of acknowledging that God is the source of all the good we do. Here we arrive at a final puzzle—not in the biblical text, but in ourselves. If we value these qualities, why don't we embody them more in our lives?

Week 4

POWER STRUGGLES

Questions to Begin

10 minutes
Use a question or two to get warmed up for the reading.

1 What gift or skill are you
especially glad to possess?

2 In what situation would you like
to be the leader, if you could?

Consider that Jesus, the apostle and high priest of our confession, was faithful to the one who appointed him, just as Moses also "was faithful in all God's house." Yet Jesus is worthy of more glory than Moses, just as the builder of a house has more honor than the house itself.

Hebrews 3:1–3

Opening the Bible

10 minutes
Read the passage aloud. Let individuals take turns reading paragraphs.

The Background

God has designated Moses as the overall leader of the Israelites and has made his brother, Aaron, high priest. Challenges to their leadership arise, however. In our first reading, we find contention over Moses' role stirred up by his own brother and sister, Aaron and Miriam. As background to this incident, it is useful to know that Moses never sought to be leader of the Israelites and tried to get out of the responsibility when God appointed him to it (Exodus 3:13–4:17). Moses has also been happy to share leadership with others (Numbers 11:16–17, 24–30).

After the challenge by Miriam and Aaron is resolved, Moses and Aaron together face challengers to their leadership. Several men infringe on Aaron's priestly role but meet with a very unhappy end (Numbers 16). In our second reading, which follows this incident, God provides a warning against such rebellions.

The Reading: Numbers 12 and 17

Hey, We're Prophets Too!

12:1 While they were at Hazeroth, Miriam and Aaron spoke against Moses because of the Cushite woman whom he had married (for he had indeed married a Cushite woman); 2 and they said, "Has the LORD spoken only through Moses? Has he not spoken through us also?" And the LORD heard it.

3 Now the man Moses was very humble,* more so than anyone else on the face of the earth.

4 Suddenly the LORD said to Moses, Aaron, and Miriam, "Come out, you three, to the tent of meeting." So the three of them came out. 5 Then the LORD came down in a pillar of cloud, and stood at the entrance of the tent, and called Aaron and Miriam; and they both came forward. 6 And he said, "Hear my words:

*Or *devout*

> When there are prophets among you,
> > I the Lord make myself known to them in visions;
> > I speak to them in dreams.
> 7 Not so with my servant Moses;
> > he is entrusted with all my house.
> 8 With him I speak face to face—
> > clearly, not in riddles;
> > and he beholds the form of the Lord.

Why then were you not afraid to speak against my servant Moses?" 9 And the anger of the Lord was kindled against them, and he departed.

10 When the cloud went away from over the tent, Miriam had become leprous,* as white as snow. And Aaron turned towards Miriam and saw that she was leprous. 11 Then Aaron said to Moses, "Oh, my lord, do not punish us for a sin that we have so foolishly committed. 12 Do not let her be like one stillborn, whose flesh is half consumed when it comes out of its mother's womb."

13 And Moses cried to the Lord, "O God, please heal her."

14 But the Lord said to Moses, "If her father had but spit in her face, would she not bear her shame for seven days? Let her be shut out of the camp for seven days, and after that she may be brought in again."

15 So Miriam was shut out of the camp for seven days; and the people did not set out on the march until Miriam had been brought in again. 16 After that the people set out from Hazeroth, and camped in the wilderness of Paran.

A Gentle Reminder

17:1 The Lord spoke to Moses, saying: 2 Speak to the Israelites, and get twelve staffs from them, one for each ancestral house, from all the leaders of their ancestral houses. Write each man's name on his staff, 3 and write Aaron's name on the staff of Levi. For there shall be one staff for the head of each ancestral house. 4 Place them in the tent of meeting before the covenant, where I meet with you. 5 And the staff of the man whom I choose shall sprout; thus I will put a

*A term for several skin diseases; precise meaning uncertain

stop to the complaints of the Israelites that they continually make against you.

6 Moses spoke to the Israelites; and all their leaders gave him staffs, one for each leader, according to their ancestral houses, twelve staffs; and the staff of Aaron was among theirs. 7 So Moses placed the staffs before the LORD in the tent of the covenant.

8 When Moses went into the tent of the covenant on the next day, the staff of Aaron for the house of Levi had sprouted. It put forth buds, produced blossoms, and bore ripe almonds. 9 Then Moses brought out all the staffs from before the LORD to all the Israelites; and they looked, and each man took his staff.

10 And the LORD said to Moses, "Put back the staff of Aaron before the covenant, to be kept as a warning to rebels, so that you may make an end of their complaints against me, or else they will die." 11 Moses did so; just as the LORD commanded him, so he did. . . .

First Impression

5 minutes
Briefly mention a question you have about the reading or one thing in it that surprised, impressed, delighted, or challenged you. No discussion! Just listen to one another's reactions.

Exploring the Theme

If participants have not read this section already, read it aloud. Otherwise go on to "Questions for Reflection and Discussion."

12. When Moses was born in Egypt, the Pharaoh was trying to kill the Israelites' male babies. To keep Moses from government agents, his mother put him in a basket along the Nile River and his older sister kept an eye on him (Exodus 2:3–4). The girl is not identified by name, but tradition has supposed that she was Miriam. In any case, the adult Miriam has been keeping an eye on her brother Moses, and she does not like what she sees. In her opinion—and brother Aaron agrees—Moses has taken on more authority than is right. The disgruntled siblings, however, launch their attack on other grounds. They complain that Moses has married a woman from Cush—present-day Sudan. It is probably not the woman's geographical or ethnic origins that Miriam and Aaron object to. Moses has taken the woman as a second wife, and Miriam and Aaron may regard this as an offense against his first wife, Zipporah. In any case, the complaint is a pretext. The real reason Miriam and Aaron are dissatisfied with their brother becomes clear in the questions they raise: "Has the Lord spoken only through Moses? Has he not spoken through us also?" (Numbers 12:2). The pair criticize Moses' marriage only to create an opening for pressing their rival claim to authority. They seem unconcerned about how Moses' Cushite wife might feel about being treated as a political football.

We are told that Moses is exceptionally "humble" (12:3). The Hebrew word does not mean "unassertive and timid" but "devoted to God, reliant on God" (see Psalm 22:26, where it is sometimes translated "poor" and is associated with seeking the Lord; Zephaniah 2:3, where it is sometimes translated "humble" and is associated with doing his commands). Being humble in this sense, Moses does not speak in self-defense (see 11:29). In Moses' view, if God wants him to stay in leadership, God will defend him.

Although the Lord declares that he speaks directly only to Moses (12:6–8), here he avoids Moses and speaks directly to Aaron and Miriam (12:5–6). Their boast that God speaks to them is fulfilled! But what God tells them is hardly what they might have hoped to hear. God declares that no one can aspire to the position that he has granted Moses (12:6–8). While God communicates with other prophets through dreams (Deuteronomy 13:1–5), visions

(1 Samuel 9:9), and other mysterious ways (Ezekiel 17:1–2), he uses no such intermediary mechanisms with Moses. God speaks to Moses "face to face" (12:8). This statement must be taken together with God's earlier statement that no one, not even Moses, can actually see his face (Exodus 33:20). In our present reading, "face to face" does not mean that Moses is literally granted a vision of God as he is; the phrase expresses directness of communication. In this sense, two people in a completely dark room can speak face to face. The point is that God has chosen Moses for a unique relationship with him and a unique role in his plans, and there is nothing anyone can do to change this.

The disease that appears on Miriam's skin (12:10) is not what we call leprosy today, that is, Hansen's disease. The description of "leprosy" in the Old Testament (Leviticus 13) better matches ailments such as psoriasis and vitiligo. Why isn't Aaron afflicted too? Perhaps it is because Miriam took the lead in the protest (she is mentioned first in Numbers 12:1). At least Aaron's plea not to punish "us" (Numbers 12:11) acknowledges that he shares in the guilt—in contrast to the golden bull incident, when Aaron never did admit that he had done anything wrong. So maybe he is making some progress here toward honest self-evaluation.

A prophet is not only God's spokesperson to the people but the people's intercessor with God—a role we have already seen Moses playing. By asking Moses to pray for Miriam, rather than praying for her himself, Aaron acknowledges that Moses alone is the prophet-intercessor whom God has appointed. Thus Moses, whom Miriam has attacked, is in a special position to intercede for her healing. In a similar way, Job's friends, after criticizing him unfairly, must rely on Job to pray that God would forgive them (Job 42:7–8). This pattern of intercession for wrongdoers by the one who has been wronged reaches its perfection in Jesus, who prays for his tormentors as he dies on the cross: "Father, forgive them; for they do not know what they are doing" (Luke 23:34).

Moses' prayer for Miriam (12:13) is so brief that some readers have detected a lack of enthusiasm on his part. But in the Hebrew, the appeal is starkly poetic. It could be translated: "No more! Heal her, I implore!"

17. It seems almost as if God himself is growing tired of the Israelites' difficult behavior. God gives directions for putting an end to challenges to Aaron as high priest with an expression of weariness: more literally in the Hebrew, God tells Moses, "I will relieve myself" of the Israelites' complaints (17:5). It is a measure of Moses' character that he cooperates readily with God's plan for confirming Aaron's priesthood, after Aaron challenged his own position as leader of the people. Clearly, Moses is more concerned with God's will being carried out than with settling a score with his brother—a further demonstration of his humility.

A recent rebellion against Aaron had collapsed in a way not likely to be soon forgotten: the rebels perished in an earthquake (Numbers 16:31–33). But God apparently feels that a further affirmation of Aaron is needed—a lasting visual reminder.

Rabbis later discussed the description of Aaron's staff: "It put forth buds, produced blossoms, and bore ripe almonds" (17:8). When Moses found the staff, they asked, was it just sprouting—and did it bud and blossom as he held it? Or were sprouts, buds, and blossoms growing on it simultaneously? In any case, the staff must be the sweetest "warning" in the Bible (17:10).

Both of these episodes remind us of the importance of God's call in selecting leaders in the Church. Whatever processes are employed in selecting leaders, whether ordained or lay, our goal should be to discern God's gifts rather than to advance human ambitions and agendas. The episodes may also, indirectly, remind us that exercising authority is not the only form of service in the community of faith. The unspoken tragedy in Miriam, Aaron, and others seeking to fill positions of leadership to which they are not called is that they thereby neglect roles of service to which they *are* called. The two incidents point us away from an unhealthy focus on power in the community of faith. Later, Jesus will rebuke disciples who are fixated on gaining positions of leadership (Mark 10:35–45). If we heed St. Paul, each of us will concentrate on identifying, developing, and using the gifts we have been given for the good of others, rather than envying those who have been given different abilities and roles (1 Corinthians 12–14).

Questions for Reflection and Discussion

45 minutes
Choose questions according to your interest and time.

1 Consider Moses' humility.
When is it appropriate to follow
his example and refrain from
defending oneself? When is it
appropriate to speak up in one's
own defense?

2 How do you participate in Jesus'
intercession for others? In what
way is intercession part of your
personal prayer? part of the
prayer of your parish?

3 Are there good reasons and bad
reasons for desiring leadership
in the Church? Is leadership in
the Church to be sought in a
different way from leadership in
other settings?

4 When have you seen the ill
effects of envy? When have you
envied? What did you learn?
What can help a person break
free from envy?

5 What effects have you seen from people spreading accusations around rather than bringing their concerns directly to the person involved? (Be careful not to spread around any personal accusations in the process of discussion!) What can be done about this problem?

6 Think of situations in which people have various kinds of authority over you (parents, employer, teacher, bishop, police . . .). Do you have an abrasive way of relating to them? an overly compliant way? Give examples of healthy ways of relating to authorities. Where do you need to grow in this area? Are there situations in which you exercise authority over other people? Do you make it easy for them to respond to you in a good way?

7 **Focus question.** Identify one gift that God has given you. What could you do to develop it? How could you put it to use for someone else's good?

Prayer to Close

10 minutes
Use this approach—or create your own!

◆ Ask someone to read aloud these lines from St. Frances Cabrini. Pause in silence. Then allow time for participants to offer short intercessory prayers for other people. End together with an Our Father.

Prayer is powerful! It fills the earth with mercy. . . . The mercy and clemency obtained through the power of prayer will always produce its generous and saving effects in people. The mercy obtained through prayer will be like a torrent coming from that immense ocean of the inexhaustible goodness of the adorable heart of Jesus. It will . . . quietly dispose those people to approach God and enter into the ark of eternal salvation.

Week 5

Is This Progress?

Questions to Begin

10 minutes
Use a question or two to get warmed up for the reading.

1 What was one influence your mother had on your father? your father on your mother? If you're married: what is one effect your spouse has had on you?

2 Scrabble players: How many words can you form using the letters in the name Phinehas? Zimri? Cozbi?

O give thanks to the Lord, for he is good . . .
who struck down great kings,
    for his steadfast love endures forever;
and killed famous kings,
    for his steadfast love endures forever. . . .

Psalm 136:1, 17–18

10 minutes
Read the passage aloud. Let individuals take turns reading
paragraphs.

The Background

As our first reading begins, the Israelites have left the desert behind and are heading across the hilly plateau east of the Dead Sea and the Jordan River. Here there is more rain, making agriculture—and a settled population—possible. The Israelites must go through this populated area in order to get to Canaan—present-day Palestine and Israel—which lies to the west. Their journey brings them into confrontation with a king named Sihon and his royal neighbor, Og.

In our second reading, the Israelites have arrived at the Jordan River. Soon they will cross over into Canaan. But while they are camping, a serious problem arises.

Aaron and Miriam do not appear in these readings. Along with most of the Israelites who came out of Egypt, they have died along the way (Numbers 20:1, 28).

The Reading: Numbers 21:21–25, 31–35; 25:1–15

Local Chieftains Block the Way

Numbers 21:21 Then Israel sent messengers to King Sihon of the Amorites, saying, 22 "Let me pass through your land; we will not turn aside into field or vineyard; we will not drink the water of any well; we will go by the King's Highway until we have passed through your territory." 23 But Sihon would not allow Israel to pass through his territory. Sihon gathered all his people together, and went out against Israel to the wilderness; he came to Jahaz, and fought against Israel. 24 Israel put him to the sword, and took possession of his land from the Arnon to the Jabbok, as far as to the Ammonites; for the boundary of the Ammonites was strong. 25 Israel took all these towns, and Israel settled in all the towns of the Amorites, in Heshbon, and in all its villages. . . .

31 Thus Israel settled in the land of the Amorites. 32 Moses sent to spy out Jazer; and they captured its villages, and dispossessed the Amorites who were there.

33 Then they turned and went up the road to Bashan; and King Og of Bashan came out against them, he and all his people, to battle at Edrei. 34 But the LORD said to Moses, "Do not be afraid of him; for I have given him into your hand, with all his people, and all his land. You shall do to him as you did to King Sihon of the Amorites, who ruled in Heshbon." 35 So they killed him, his sons, and all his people, until there was no survivor left; and they took possession of his land.

Local Women Promote Their Gods

25:1 While Israel was staying at Shittim, the people began to have sexual relations with the women of Moab. 2 These invited the people to the sacrifices of their gods, and the people ate and bowed down to their gods. 3 Thus Israel yoked itself to the Baal of Peor, and the LORD's anger was kindled against Israel. 4 The LORD said to Moses, "Take all the chiefs of the people, and impale them in the sun before the LORD, in order that the fierce anger of the LORD may turn away from Israel." 5 And Moses said to the judges of Israel, "Each of you shall kill any of your people who have yoked themselves to the Baal of Peor."

6 Just then one of the Israelites came and brought a Midianite woman into his family, in the sight of Moses and in the sight of the whole congregation of the Israelites, while they were weeping at the entrance of the tent of meeting. 7 When Phinehas son of Eleazar, son of Aaron the priest, saw it, he got up and left the congregation. Taking a spear in his hand, 8 he went after the Israelite man into the tent, and pierced the two of them, the Israelite and the woman, through the belly. So the plague was stopped among the people of Israel. 9 Nevertheless those that died by the plague were twenty-four thousand.

10 The LORD spoke to Moses, saying: 11 "Phinehas son of Eleazar, son of Aaron the priest, has turned back my wrath from the Israelites by manifesting such zeal among them on my behalf that in my jealousy I did not consume the Israelites. 12 Therefore say, 'I hereby grant him my covenant of peace. 13 It shall be for him and for his descendants after him a covenant of perpetual priesthood,

because he was zealous for his God, and made atonement for the Israelites.'"

14 The name of the slain Israelite man, who was killed with the Midianite woman, was Zimri son of Salu, head of an ancestral house belonging to the Simeonites. 15 The name of the Midianite woman who was killed was Cozbi daughter of Zur, who was the head of a clan, an ancestral house in Midian.

First Impression

5 minutes
Briefly mention a question you have about the reading or one thing in it that surprised, impressed, delighted, or challenged you. No discussion! Just listen to one another's reactions.

Exploring the Theme

If participants have not read this section already, read it aloud. Otherwise go on to "Questions for Reflection and Discussion."

21. The incidents involving Sihon and Og sound like ethnic slaughters, but may actually have been something different. Sihon is an Amorite (Numbers 21:21). The Amorites are thought to have been foreign warriors who came into the area east of the Jordan River and subjugated the existing population a generation or two before the Israelites arrived. The "people" that Sihon gathers together (21:23) are probably his Amorite soldiers, not the local farmers and shepherds (the Hebrew word can mean both *people* and *troops*). Thus it is the kings and their military forces that the Israelites kill, not the general population.

Scholars speculate that the peasants who had been ruled by Sihon and Og may then have joined the Israelites' covenant with God. The Bible contains an account of a later ceremony renewing the covenant between God and the people of Israel that may have been an opportunity for other people, like the former subjects of Sihon and Og, to express their allegiance (Joshua 24). Belonging to the Israelite community would be a great improvement over living under Sihon and Og. The Israelite community was based on the principle that God is king, and God is not like a human warlord: his laws prescribe justice and forbid exploitation.

In a history of the world's military exploits, the Israelites' victories over Sihon and Og wouldn't rate a footnote. Sihon and Og may have seemed fearsome to the Israelites, but they ruled miniature kingdoms. One estimate of the number of soldiers at the service of each of these kinglets: less than a hundred! Nevertheless, the Israelites' victories over them are significant, because they were professional troops, while the Israelites were untrained for warfare. The Israelites' decision to defend themselves rather than flee was based on trust in God's help. In facing these kings, the Israelites overcame the fear that had paralyzed them in the past (Numbers 13–14).

25. While the Israelites are camping on the east bank of the Jordan River, some of the men get to know the local women. The nature of the relationships that develop is unclear. Perhaps the Israelite men take Moabite women as concubines; perhaps they marry them. In any case, the author focuses not on the sexual relationship but on the consequence of it: Israelite men begin to worship the Moabites' gods (25:3).

The main local deity is called Baal of Peor—Baal meaning "lord" or "master," and Peor being a place name. Baal of Peor is the supposed divine power that brings fertility to plants and animals in the area where the Israelites are camping. Other Baals are worshipped throughout the region that the Israelites have now entered. For the Israelites, who have been living in the wilderness, these agricultural fertility gods are something new—and something for which they are unprepared. Perhaps, the Israelites think, in this new land it would be prudent not to offend the local gods, lest they hold back the rain. This attitude, of course, is totally unacceptable to the God of Israel, who rightly calls for exclusive loyalty, since he is the only source of life.

God orders Moses to "impale" (25:4) the leaders who have let the people drift into idolatry. Scholars disagree on the meaning of the Hebrew word, but whatever its precise meaning, it seems to refer to some ghastly form of execution. Moses' command (25:5), however, does not match God's directive. Furthermore, no one takes any action whatsoever; they just stand around weeping (25:6). The carefully organized camp pictured in our readings in Week 2 seems to have fallen apart. Some Israelites turn to new gods; others do nothing to correct them. Harsh penalties are proposed; but, in fact, nothing is done. Moses has become a passive observer (25:6).

While Moses and other Israelites are bemoaning the situation, an Israelite man named Zimri makes a public display of unfaithfulness to God. He brings a Moabite woman named Cozbi into the camp, introduces her to his family, and proceeds to marry her in front of everyone. Presumably, worship of her god, Baal of Peor, will soon follow.

The New Revised Standard Version of Numbers 25:8 says that Phinehas follows the couple and stabs them "through the belly," apparently while they are having sex. But the Hebrew text can be given a different translation. The meaning may be that the couple go into a ceremonial tent, or canopy, and are attacked there by Phinehas, who stabs them "at the marriage canopy," where they are performing some ritual action. Either way, Phinehas's action is shocking. More shocking is God's approval (25:10–13). But later biblical tradition shows signs of reevaluation. Psalm 106 states that "Phinehas stood up and interceded, and the plague was stopped. And that has been reckoned to him as righteousness" (Psalm 106:30–31). Notice that the psalmist omits any mention of Phinehas stabbing the couple; he commends Phinehas not for murderous "zeal," as in Numbers 25:10, but for mediation through prayer (he "interceded" with God). The psalmist, it seems, is implicitly delivering a negative judgment on Phinehas's angry deed. Later, Jesus, by his whole life and teaching, makes it clear that we are to help each other be faithful to God not through violence or threats but through love and good example. (See also the introduction, page 13.)

The episode shows that temptations to be unfaithful to God plagued the Israelites from the beginning to the end of their journey. "You shall have no other gods before me," God told them before they set out (Exodus 20:3). Yet while they were still at Mount Sinai, they made a false image for worship. They end their journey by making offerings to Baal of Peor. Haven't they made any progress at all in the course of their travels? Perhaps a little. The golden bull debacle seems to have taught them not to make golden bulls, but now the invitation to worship Baal of Peor catches them off guard. They were prepared to meet the challenge of yesterday but not the challenge of today. And, for all its harshness, Phinehas's act may give a glimmer of hope. Even though he is a long way from grasping how best to help others remain faithful to God, Phinehas, in contrast to his grandfather Aaron (Exodus 32:2–5), takes action against idolatry. Perhaps some of the new generation has learned a lesson that the older generation did not.

In any case, the Israelites' repeated unfaithfulness to God despite the marvels God performed alerts us to the fact that, however far we have traveled with the Lord, it is always possible for us to part ways from him. The Israelites' experience, then, warns us not to be complacent about our loyalty to God but to root ourselves in God's life day by day.

45 minutes
Choose questions according to your interest and time.

1 What problems in your life need to be met with courage? How can you grow in trusting that God will help you deal with them?

2 Where do gospel values meet resistance or opposition in society today? Where do Christians need to grow in facing this opposition with courage? with love? with humility? How has your understanding of how to fight for what is right developed?

3 What aspects of contemporary culture harmonize with God's purposes? How can Christians strengthen these aspects of society?

4 In your own life, what temptations to compromise with unchristian values and practices do you find the most difficult to deal with? How can Christians support each other in growing in faithfulness to Jesus—in the family? in schools? in parishes? in work situations? elsewhere? What are appropriate and inappropriate ways of helping one another be faithful?

5 Many people think that older folks are more religious than younger ones. Is this necessarily true? Do you see signs that the younger generation in the Church today may do better in some ways than the older generation has?

6 **Focus question.** Is there a problem in your own life, family, parish, or city, where you have been hanging back rather than taking action? What action should you take? What are you waiting for?

Prayer to Close

10 minutes
Use this approach—or create your own!

◆   Let one person read the
following reflection aloud. Pause
in silence. Then pray Psalm
119:73–80, 129–135. End with
a Glory to the Father.

St. Philip Neri composed short
prayers that he said often during
the day. Among his favorites:
"My Jesus, don't trust me."
"I distrust myself, but I trust
in you, my Jesus." "My Jesus,
if you forget me, I will surely
forget you." "My Jesus, if you
don't help me, I'm ruined." What
do you think of his attitude?
Is it realistic? exaggerated?
something you can learn from?

FAREWELL

Questions to Begin

10 minutes
Use a question or two to get warmed up for the reading.

1 What's your usual way of saying good-bye?
❏ Hugs and kisses. Then more hugs and kisses.
❏ A new conversation at the door.
❏ Waving good-bye until everyone is out of sight.
❏ A handshake and a smile.
❏ "So long" is long enough.

2 Where would you like to die?

He has placed before you fire and water;
stretch out your hand for whichever you choose.
Before each person are life and death,
and whichever one chooses will be given.

Sirach 15:16–17

Opening the Bible

10 minutes
*Read the passage aloud. Let individuals take turns reading
paragraphs.*

The Background

The Israelites are still camping east of the Jordan River, waiting for
the signal to cross over into Canaan. Their wait provides the perfect
opportunity for them to look back over their journey and gather up
lessons to be learned before moving on and becoming preoccupied
with the new challenges they will face on the other side of the river.
In a couple of long sermons—they take up almost the entire book of
Deuteronomy—Moses leads the people in a review of their journey.
(As they sit in the sweltering heat, do they wish he would speak
more briefly?) Our second reading contains excerpts from these
sermons.

   For Moses, the sermon is not just the discharge of a
pastoral responsibility. It is his farewell, for God has told him that
his death is near (our first reading). The people will continue on
into the land God has prepared for them, but Moses will no longer
accompany them. He has lived a long life; indeed, virtually three
lives, having spent forty years as a member of pharaoh's household,
forty as a shepherd in the wilderness of Sinai, and forty as the
leader of the people. Now he has reached the end of his personal
journey (our third reading).

The Reading: Numbers 27:12–20; Deuteronomy 3:23–27; 30:15–20; 31:1–6; 34:1–8

God Tells Moses His Death Is Near

Numbers 27:12 The LORD said to Moses, "Go up this mountain of the
Abarim range, and see the land that I have given to the Israelites.
13 When you have seen it, you also shall be gathered to your people,
as your brother Aaron was, 14 because you rebelled against my word
in the wilderness of Zin when the congregation quarreled with me.
You did not show my holiness before their eyes." . . .
   15 Moses spoke to the LORD, saying, 16 "Let the LORD, the
God of the spirits of all flesh, appoint someone over the congregation

[17] who shall go out before them and come in before them, who shall lead them out and bring them in, so that the congregation of the LORD may not be like sheep without a shepherd."

[18] So the LORD said to Moses, "Take Joshua son of Nun, a man in whom is the spirit, and lay your hand upon him; [19] have him stand before Eleazar the priest and all the congregation, and commission him in their sight. [20] You shall give him some of your authority, so that all the congregation of the Israelites may obey."

Sound Bites from Moses' Final Sermon

Deuteronomy 3:23 I entreated the LORD, saying: [24] "O Lord GOD, you have only begun to show your servant your greatness and your might; what god in heaven or on earth can perform deeds and mighty acts like yours! [25] Let me cross over to see the good land beyond the Jordan, that good hill country and the Lebanon." [26] But the LORD was angry with me on your account and would not heed me. The LORD said to me, "Enough from you! Never speak to me of this matter again! [27] Go up to the top of Pisgah and look around you to the west, to the north, to the south, and to the east. Look well, for you shall not cross over this Jordan." . . .

30:15 See, I have set before you today life and prosperity, death and adversity. [16] If you obey the commandments of the LORD your God that I am commanding you today, by loving the LORD your God, walking in his ways, and observing his commandments, decrees, and ordinances, then you shall live and become numerous, and the LORD your God will bless you in the land that you are entering to possess. [17] But if your heart turns away and you do not hear, but are led astray to bow down to other gods and serve them, [18] I declare to you today that you shall perish; you shall not live long in the land that you are crossing the Jordan to enter and possess. [19] I call heaven and earth to witness against you today that I have set before you life and death, blessings and curses. Choose life so that you and your descendants may live, [20] loving the LORD your God, obeying him, and holding fast to him; for that means life to you and length of days, so that you may live in the land that the LORD swore to give to your ancestors, to Abraham, to Isaac, and to Jacob.

31:1 When Moses had finished speaking all these words to all Israel, 2 he said to them: "I am now one hundred twenty years old. I am no longer able to get about, and the LORD has told me, 'You shall not cross over this Jordan.' 3 The LORD your God himself will cross over before you. He will destroy these nations before you, and you shall dispossess them. Joshua also will cross over before you, as the LORD promised. 4 The LORD will do to them as he did to Sihon and Og, the kings of the Amorites, and to their land, when he destroyed them. 5 The LORD will give them over to you and you shall deal with them in full accord with the command that I have given to you. 6 Be strong and bold; have no fear or dread of them, because it is the LORD your God who goes with you; he will not fail you or forsake you."

The Death of Moses

34:1 Then Moses went up from the plains of Moab to Mount Nebo, to the top of Pisgah, which is opposite Jericho, and the LORD showed him the whole land: Gilead as far as Dan, 2 all Naphtali, the land of Ephraim and Manasseh, all the land of Judah as far as the Western Sea, 3 the Negeb, and the Plain—that is, the valley of Jericho, the city of palm trees—as far as Zoar. 4 The LORD said to him, "This is the land of which I swore to Abraham, to Isaac, and to Jacob, saying, 'I will give it to your descendants'; I have let you see it with your eyes, but you shall not cross over there."

5 Then Moses, the servant of the LORD, died there in the land of Moab, at the LORD's command. 6 He was buried in a valley in the land of Moab, opposite Beth-peor, but no one knows his burial place to this day. 7 Moses was one hundred twenty years old when he died; his sight was unimpaired and his vigor had not abated. 8 The Israelites wept for Moses in the plains of Moab thirty days; then the period of mourning for Moses was ended.

First Impression

5 minutes
Briefly mention a question you have about the reading or one thing in it that surprised, impressed, delighted, or challenged you. No discussion! Just listen to one another's reactions.

Exploring the Theme

If participants have not read this section already, read it aloud. Otherwise go on to "Questions for Reflection and Discussion."

Numbers 27. Moses has demonstrated his deep-rooted concern for the people throughout their long journey—even if they have sometimes totally exasperated him. So it is not surprising that he responds to God's warning of his approaching death with a businesslike request that God would appoint someone to succeed him as leader of the people. Moses' pastoral concern is to be expected. Yet we may wonder why he doesn't express any appeal against God's ruling that he will not enter Canaan with the people— or even any sign of dismay. Has Moses grown too old to care?

Deuteronomy 3, 30, 31. Knowing that his end is near, Moses offers the people some final words of advice, reviewing with them what God has done for them and what God promises to do and reminding them of God's instructions for their life together as a people. In essence, Moses' final sermon is an encouragement to trust and obey God. The famous passage about loving God with all one's being—"the greatest and first commandment," Jesus will call it (Matthew 22:37–38)—is contained in this sermon (Deuteronomy 6:5).

In his sermon, Moses strikes the personal note that was missing in the preceding reading from Numbers 27. He recounts his appeal to God to let him enter the land (Deuteronomy 3:23–27). So he has not grown too old to care! It is easy to imagine his line of thought: *If I am to die now, can't I at least die on the other side of the river, in that 'good land' toward which I have been journeying for forty years?* But it is not to be. God has barred Moses from the land because of his failure to trust and honor God at Meribah (Numbers 20:12; 27:14). When we consider Moses' age—he is now 120 years old—it seems that the limitations of the human organism also rule out any further journeying.

After a lengthy review of God's instructions, Moses reminds the Israelites that obedience to God is not merely the condition for obtaining the good life; it *is* the good life (Deuteronomy 30). The fundamental gift that God is offering is not land on which to make a home but the opportunity to live according to his will—and his help to do so. If they enjoy good things in Canaan but choose a

way of life other than the one God has laid out for them, they will
choose an existence that is not truly life, not truly happy. Drawing
on the experience of a lifetime, Moses urges the younger generation
to choose God as they face new situations. To choose God is to
choose life. On this note, Moses brings his great sermon to a close
(Deuteronomy 30:19–20).

No response by the people is recorded. This stands in
contrast to an earlier episode, at Mount Sinai, when Moses set
the Lord's requirements before the people and they declared, "All
the words that the Lord has spoken we will do" (Exodus 24:3).
Soon after that episode, in the incident with the golden bull, they
broke their promise. Perhaps now they make no verbal response to
Moses' words because they have they learned that it is not what
they say but what they do that will count. Biblical scholar Patrick
Miller observes that "the effect of the silence of the text at this
point is to leave the decision open. The response is not reported
as a past act. It is to be given by those who read and hear these
words—today." Rather than focusing our attention on what the
Israelites might have said, the author, by his silence on the matter,
has left Moses' sermon hanging in the air as a challenge to us,
the readers. Each of us is invited to ask ourselves what Moses'
summons to choose God means for us—and to make our response.

At Mount Sinai, Moses' absence raised the Israelites'
anxieties. The golden bull was, in part, a substitute for their absent
leader. Now Moses announces to the people that he is leaving them
forever (Deuteronomy 31). Will anxiety come rushing in again? Not if
they remember their experiences of God on their journey. The most
basic lesson to be learned from their journey is simply this: *God
is with us.* If they hold on to this lesson, they will be able to face a
change in leadership, and every other change, with courage. Thus,
Moses' valedictory to them: "Be strong and bold; have no fear or
dread of them, because it is the Lord your God who goes with you;
he will not fail you or forsake you" (Deuteronomy 31:6).

Significantly, this encouragement is given not just to Joshua
but to everyone. Certainly Joshua, the people's leader, will need

courage (31:7). Not only the leader, however, but the whole people must be brave.

Deuteronomy 34. Moses now goes up a mountain for the last time. From a west-facing spur near the peak of Mount Nebo, he looks out over the Jordan River valley at the land of Canaan. He does not look unaided: "The Lord showed him," the biblical author tells us (Deuteronomy 34:1), which explains how Moses sees much more than the unaided eye can see from Mount Nebo, even on a clear day.

The author calls Moses the "servant" of God (34:5). This modest word was used in the ancient Near East for important government officials (compare the way *secretary* is used for members of the president's cabinet in the United States). Moses was God's trusted, intimate, and beloved servant.

The author's assessment of Moses' condition—"his vigor had not abated" (Deuteronomy 34:7) seems to conflict with Moses' own statement that he is "no longer able to get about" (Deuteronomy 31:2). But the Hebrew text more literally states that Moses' "moisture had not departed," that is, he was not dried out. Moses was not as wrinkled as one might expect a hundred-twenty-year-old man to be. But even if Moses did not look his age, he felt it, as he himself makes clear (Deuteronomy 31:2).

Moses died "at the Lord's command" (Deuteronomy 34:5). In the Hebrew text, this is expressed literally as "at God's mouth." In rabbinic tradition, this was interpreted as meaning that Moses died at a kiss from God. For this reason, the term "death by a kiss" is sometimes used by Jews to refer to the passing of one who is taken quickly and painlessly in old age. Thus ended the life of God's greatest servant before the coming of his Son.

Questions for Reflection and Discussion

45 minutes
Choose questions according to your interest and time.

1 Where do you face a decision that in some sense involves choosing for or against God? What help do you need to make the right decision and carry through on it?

2 Among people you have known personally, who stands as an example of what it means to follow the Lord throughout a long life? What can you learn from this person?

3 What one or two saints in the history of the Church seem to you especially appropriate as models for the Church today? How do you think we could imitate them?

4 If you knew you were about to die, what aspects of your life would you wish to put in order now? What wisdom from your experience would you like to share with those who are close to you—especially with those who are younger? What would you encourage them to do?

5 Where and when do you feel anxiety or fear? When you do, do you remind yourself of God's presence? What incidents in your life have taught you about recognizing God's presence? Do you recall them when you are facing difficulties?

6 What events in the life of the Church in the past stand as reminders of Jesus' promise to be present among his followers always (Matthew 28:20)?

7 **Focus question.** What is the most important lesson for you in the readings over the last six weeks? What is the most important message for the Church today in these readings? How do you think the Church should respond? What can you do to contribute to its response?

Prayer to Close

10 minutes
Use this approach—or create your own!

◆ Pray this prayer together. Give an opportunity for any brief prayers that participants may wish to offer. Close with an Our Father.

Lord, you set before us a choice between life and death, between you, the giver of life, and life without you, which is not really life at all. Help us to choose you. Help us to understand what it means to choose you in the changing circumstances of our lives. Do not let our hearts be led astray from you. Fill our hearts more and more with your love—with love for you and love for the people around us. Help us to hold fast to you. Help your whole Church to hold fast to you.

Suggestions for Bible Discussion Groups

Like a camping trip, a Bible discussion group works best if you agree on where you're going and how you intend to get there. Many groups use their first meeting to talk over such questions. Here is a checklist of issues, with bits of advice from people who have experience in Bible discussions. (A planning discussion will go more smoothly if the leaders have thought through the following issues beforehand.)

Agree on your purpose. Are you getting together to gain wisdom and direction for your lives? to finally get acquainted with the Bible? to support one another in following Christ? to encourage those who are exploring—or reexploring—the Church? for other reasons?

Agree on attitudes. For example: "We're all beginners here." "We're here to help one another understand and respond to God's word." "We're not here to offer counseling or direction to one another." "We want to read Scripture prayerfully." What do *you* wish to emphasize? Make it explicit!

Agree on ground rules. Barbara J. Fleischer, in her useful book *Facilitating for Growth,* recommends that a group clearly state its approach to the following:

- *Preparation.* Do we agree to read the material and prepare answers to the questions before each meeting?
- *Attendance.* What kind of priority will we give to our meetings?
- *Self-revelation.* Are we willing to help the others in the group gradually get to know us—our weaknesses as well as our strengths, our needs as well as our gifts?
- *Listening.* Will we commit ourselves to listen to one another?
- *Confidentiality.* Will we keep everything that is shared *with* the group *in* the group?
- *Discretion.* Will we refrain from sharing about the faults and sins of people who are not in the group?
- *Encouragement and support.* Will we give as well as receive?
- *Participation.* Will we give each person the time and opportunity to make a contribution?

You could probably take a pen and draw a circle around *listening* and *confidentiality.* Those two points are especially important.

The following items could be added to Fleischer's list:

◆ *Relationship with parish.* Is our group part of the adult faith-formation program? independent but operating with the express approval of the pastor? not a parish-based group?

◆ *New members.* Will we let new members join us once we have begun the six weeks of discussions?

Agree on housekeeping.

◆ *When will we meet?*

◆ *How often will we meet?* Meeting weekly or every other week is best if you can manage it. William Riley remarks, "Meetings once a month are too distant from each other for the threads of the last session not to be lost" *(The Bible Study Group: An Owner's Manual).*

◆ *How long will each meeting run?*

◆ *Where will we meet?*

◆ *Is any setup needed?* Christine Dodd writes that "the problem with meeting in a place like a church hall is that it can be very soul-destroying," given the cold, impersonal feel of many church facilities. If you have to meet in a church facility, Dodd recommends doing something to make the area homey *(Making Scripture Work).*

◆ *Who will host the meetings?* Leaders and hosts are not necessarily the same people.

◆ *Will we have refreshments?* Who will provide them? Don Cousins and Judson Poling make this recommendation: "Serve refreshments if you like, but save snacks and other foods for the end of the meeting to minimize distractions" *(Leader's Guide 1).*

◆ *What about child care?* Most experienced leaders of Bible discussion groups discourage bringing infants or other children to adult Bible discussions.

Agree on leadership. You need someone to facilitate—to keep the discussion on track, to see that everyone has a chance to speak, to help the group stay on schedule. Rena Duff, editor of the newsletter *Sharing God's Word Today,* recommends having two or three people take turns leading the discussions.

It's okay if the leader is not an expert on the Bible. You have this Six Weeks book as a guide, and if questions come up that no one can answer, you can delegate a participant to do a little research between meetings. Perhaps your parish priest or someone on the pastoral staff of your parish could offer advice. Or help may be available from your diocesan catechetical office or a local Catholic college or seminary.

It's important for the leader to set an example of listening, to draw out the quieter members (and occasionally restrain the more vocal ones), to move the group on when it gets stuck, to get the group back on track when the discussion moves away from the topic, and to restate and summarize what the group is learning. Sometimes the leader needs to remind the members of their agreements. An effective group leader is enthusiastic about the topic and the discussions and sets an example of learning from others and of using resources for growing in understanding.

As a discussion group matures, other members of the group will increasingly share in doing all these things on their own initiative.

Bible discussion is an opportunity to experience the fulfillment of Jesus' promise "Where two or three are gathered in my name, I am there among them" (Matthew 18:20). Put your discussion group in Jesus' hands. Pray for the guidance of the Spirit. And have a great time exploring God's word together!

Suggestions for Individuals

Y ou can use this book just as well for individual study as for group discussion. While discussing the Bible with other people can be a rich experience, there are advantages to reading on your own. For example:

◆ You can focus on the points that interest you most.

◆ You can go at your own pace.

◆ You can be completely relaxed and unashamedly honest in your answers to all the questions, since you don't have to share them with anyone!

My suggestions for using this book on your own are these:

◆ Don't skip "Questions to Begin" or "First Impression."

◆ Take your time on "Questions for Reflection and Discussion." While a group will probably not have enough time to work on all the questions, you can allow yourself the time to consider all of them if you are using the book by yourself.

◆ After reading "Exploring the Theme," go back and reread the Scripture text before answering the Questions for Reflection and Discussion.

◆ Take the time to look up all the parenthetical Scripture references.

◆ Read additional sections of Scripture related to the excerpts in this book. For example, read the portions of Scripture that come before and after the sections that form the readings in this Six Weeks book. You will understand the readings better by viewing them in context in the Bible.

◆ Since you control the pace, give yourself plenty of opportunities to reflect on the meaning of the Scripture passages for you. Let your reading be an opportunity for these words to become God's words to you.

Bibles

The following editions of the Bible contain the full set of biblical books recognized by the Catholic Church, along with a great deal of useful explanatory material:

- The Catholic Study Bible (Oxford University Press), which uses the text of the New American Bible
- The Catholic Bible: Personal Study Edition (Oxford University Press), which also uses the text of the New American Bible
- The New Jerusalem Bible, the regular (not the reader's) edition (Doubleday)

Books, Web Sites, and Other Resources

- Stephen J. Binz, *The God of Freedom and Life: A Commentary on the Book of Exodus* (Collegeville, MN: Liturgical Press, 1994).
- Katharine Doob Sakenfeld, *Journeying with God: A Commentary on the Book of Numbers* (Grand Rapids, MI: William B. Eerdmans Publishing Company, 1995).
- Patrick D. Miller, *Deuteronomy* (Louisville, KY: John Knox Press, 1990).
- Saint Maria Faustina Kowalska, *Diary of Saint Maria Faustina Kowalska: Divine Mercy in My Soul* (Stockbridge, MA: Marian Press, 2005).
- George W. Kosicki, C. S. B., *Meet Saint Faustina: Herald of Divine Mercy* (Ann Arbor, MI: Charis Books, 2001).
- Antoinette Bosco, *One Day He Beckoned* (Notre Dame, IN: Ave Maria Press, 2004).

How has Scripture had an impact on your life? Was this book helpful to you in your study of the Bible? Please send comments, suggestions, and personal experiences to Kevin Perrotta, General Editor, Editorial Department, Loyola Press, 3441 N. Ashland Ave., Chicago, IL 60657.